Thriving In Turbulent Times

With Contributions From 8 World Famous Leaders

Hosted by
Raymond Aaron

World Prosper Summit
April 24 & 25, 2020
Day 2 of 2

10-10-10
Publishing

Thriving in Turbulent Times – Series 2 (Raw unedited - Day 2 of 2)

www.WorldProsperSummit.com/livestream

Limits of Liability and Disclaimer of Warranty

The author and publisher shall not be liable for your misuse of the enclosed material. This book is strictly for informational and educational purposes only. Content and wording have been transcribed from a live event and is raw unedited version, product was presented at the time of the event.

Warning – Disclaimer

The purpose of this book is to educate and entertain. The author and/or publisher do not guarantee that anyone following these techniques, suggestions, tips, ideas, or strategies will become successful. The author and/or publisher shall have neither liability nor responsibility to anyone with respect to any loss or damage caused, or alleged to be caused, directly or indirectly by the information contained in this book.

Publisher
10-10-10 Publishing
Markham, ON
Canada

Printed in Canada and the United States of America

Table of Contents

How to Manage Your Mindset, Focus, and Emotions During This Crazy Time

John Assaraf

Raymond Aaron:

Hello and John's is here, when he says something it's just flat out true. He doesn't exaggerate. He doesn't spin. He just says it. I love that. If you hear in his presentation that something's difficult, it is. If he says something's easy, it is. Not just easy for him or easy for smart guys. He tells the truth and I love that about him. I haven't hugged you in a long time, so whenever we're-

John Assaraf:

Virtual hug maybe. Virtual hug.

Raymond Aaron:

Whenever we're allowed to hug, none of this elbow bump, whenever we're allowed to hug again, I'll stand on a stool because you're so much taller than me and we'll have a big hug. Okay, take it away.

John Assaraf:

Thanks Raymond. It's a pleasure to be here with everybody, and if all of you are ready to have an amazing time type in the chat right now, "Let's rock this house today," and we want you to share this all over the internet, and let's lift as we climb. Right? We're all climbing, trying to figure this out. Let's lift each other as we climb.

I wanted to share with you just a little bit about what's happening in our brains right now. A lot of people are talking about coronavirus, life after coronavirus. Well guess what? There isn't life after coronavirus. There's only life with coronavirus until we find a vaccine because we have almost eight billion inhabitants of Earth. Unless everybody gets it and develops the immunity towards it, we have to live with coronavirus.

John Assaraf:

I want to just share with you a couple things that may be going on in your brain, and I'll give you some tools. I call them innercise, and they're based on my new bestselling book, and I believe Raymond's going to give you guys a gift based on that later on. How many of you agree that especially in times of chaos, mindset is what separates the best from the rest? If you agree, just type in there, "John or Raymond, yes I agree." I'm going to give you a few tools to manage your mindset and your emotions so that you can navigate through this pandemic in a calm way versus in a reactive stressful way. If that sounds like something you love, let's do that because I believe that mindset is what separates the best from the rest.

Let's understand what's happening right now. Never in the history of our species have we been faced with what's going on right now. Never has every human being had this threat at their door that has activated the threat response part of their brain where there's a predator that might get them or has gotten them. Never has that threat also possibly going to lead to death. Real death. Not imagined death. Not kind of sort of maybe, but real. Would you all agree that there's this predator called coronavirus 19 or COVID-19, that if you get it there's a chance you may die. Of course. What is that doing to yours and my brain? What is happening when this high state of alert is going on? Television, radio, internet, me talking about it, Raymond talking about it, other speakers talk about it. Everybody is talking about this and how everything in one week changed. Everything changed. Not because you wanted it to, because you planned it. Everything changed because of this thing called the coronavirus.

John Assaraf:

What is happening in yours and my brain? First, understand that the number one and number two priorities of your brain and my brain is survival above all else. We've been walking Earth for two and a half million years and our brain has been wiring itself for survival of the species above else. Right below that is avoidance of pain or discomfort. That's why we are creatures of comfort, creatures of habits. Our brain is wired at the very, very base of the brain stem for these two things. But it also, because of number one and two, it wants to conserve energy. It is an energy miser not wanting us to get out of our comfort zone, not wanting us to change the way we think or the way we feel or even our expectations. Then once one, two and three are done, then it says, great, and what can I eat? What can I have sex with? How can I gain pleasure? How can I have fun?

3

John Assaraf:

When our brain is doing this every single moment of every day to make sure that we have safety, mental safety, emotional safety, physical safety, and right now with 26 million Americans and I'm not sure how many in Australia or Asia or in Europe or anywhere else in the world, but when we have 26 million Americans out of work, when real estate prices are going to start plummeting, when interest rates are low but the stock market is volatile, we are having a pandemic on every single front of our species biology.

John Assaraf:

What does that do? What does it do to you and me is this, and I'm going to show you how to manage this because if you don't manage it, you will be reacting abruptly instead of responding calmly. Let me repeat. Without knowing how to manage this you'll be reacting abruptly instead of managing calmly. When we have the fight, flight or freeze part of our brain activated, I also call that the Frankenstein brain. The Frankenstein brain is the part of you that starts to have self doubt and you start to question what am I doing? What should I do? Am I safe? Am I not safe? When you start to have self doubt there's a lot of uncertainty. Now when there's a lot of uncertainty, will I have a job? How will my business do? Should I start a business? Should I not start a business? Should I change careers? Should I do something differently? What if I run out of money? What if, what if negatives. Whenever our Frankenstein brain is activated, we are in this disempowering pattern that causes us to worry incestuously.

Now I want you to understand something. When we have real threat, this is triggered at an unconscious level and this is releasing the neurochemical called cortisol or epinephrine or norepinephrine, the stress response chemicals that causes this high state of anxiety even if we're not aware of it. It's this current that's running beneath the surface of everything and it triggers the fear response part of our brain. The fear response part of our brain that's responsible to make sure that we survive, to make sure that we avoid pain or discomfort, and to make sure that we are safe if all of a sudden on high, high, high alert. If we don't know how to manage this, we can actually see the blood flow shifting from what I'm going to show you in just a moment, the Einstein part of the brain, the left prefrontal cortex, it shifts blood flow away from the thinking part of the brain, the imagination part of the brain. The part of our brain that can help us figure out how to take advantage of this pandemic instead of being a victim of it in a fearful, stressful state.

John Assaraf:

Our thinking brain is focusing on all of the negative potential consequences instead of all of the possible amazing successes that you can have right now. When you're inner Frankenstein is active, it is what sabotages your ability to focus on all of the potential solutions right now.

Let me give you an example. One of my clients, Linda, she is a Pilates instructor. For 30 years she's had a studio in a small town in Canada. All of a sudden six weeks ago she's like, "John, what am I supposed to do? I'm going to lose my business. I'm going to lose my clients." She was in this Frankenstein brain talking negatively about all the potential negative things that could happen, might happen, et cetera. I let her talk about all that stuff for several minutes and then I said to her, "Linda, let's just shift over to the other side for just a moment. What if you could figure this out? What if there's a solution in here somewhere? What if you can actually recalibrate your business so that you don't have to be working all day long with private clients in your studio? What if." We start to recalibrate some of her thinking, and I'll show you in just a moment how we did that.

John Assaraf:

Guess what happened? She actually took all of her equipment within three days and she brought it to her top clients' homes. She set it up for them. She had her husband set it up for them. She started to do virtual private lessons with her clients. She also took on a side business to create coronavirus masks with her company logo on them and she gave them to all of her clients and then she sold 2,000 of them outside her studio before everybody was self quarantined, and she's like, "Oh my God. I'm able to actually make more money as a Pilates instructor that had a studio before."

Did she get innovative? Absolutely. Did she get creative? Absolutely. But in a state of panic and fear and worry and stress, she would have gone downhill very, very fast. By flipping the switch from anxiety, stress and fear that led to her lack of control, that led to her hyper focusing on the negative, led her to start thinking that she was a victim, to having these disempowered feeling and powerlessness and reactiveness and destructive behaviors and pain and suffering, she learned how to have mental and emotional control in chaotic times.

John Assaraf:

I want you to understand something. God created your brain and it is worth, I don't know, a quintillion dollar because we can't even replicate it. Now part of the challenge is if you don't know how to use it really well, then you're a victim of your old conditioning. How do you have more mental and emotional control when you need it? That is by learning how to activate your inner Einstein. There's nothing wrong with Frankenstein. Frankenstein is your early warning detection mechanism and Frankenstein is there to protect you, to help you survive. It's no different than having gas pedal on your car and a brake. Gas pedal go, break stop. If you have both of them on at the same time there's a lot of motion but you're not getting anywhere very, very fast.

John Assaraf:

I want you to remember something about your Frankenstein brain. Imagine you're driving your car and all of a sudden there's a light that pops up on the dash. Do you ever take a hammer and hit the light? Of course not. The light is nothing more than a signal. Maybe you're low on windshield washer fluid. Maybe your back right tire is low. Maybe the trunk hood or the trunk is open. Your fear center, all of the what if signals that are negative or disempowering are nothing more than signals that are coming up from your memory bank, your implicit memory bank, and giving you a signal to be aware of.

John Assaraf:

Now in the absence of mental and emotional control, those signals appear real. The neurochemicals are real in your body and you have these feelings that you don't like. But any emotion, the energy that's in motion in your body, a feeling, which is the end result of a trigger in your subconscious mind, will only last 90 seconds if you observe it instead of reliving that possibility over and over and over again, thereby creating a self-fulfilling disempowering or negative [inaudible 00:12:50]. Your inner Einstein, I'm going to show you how to deactivate one and activate the other one in just a moment.

John Assaraf:

Your inner Einstein is the genius part of your brain. It's the GPS part of your brain. It's the left prefrontal cortex that is this part of your brain that is capable of helping you achieve any goal that you want. Any goal that you want. Instead of having a negative disempowering imagination, how do you focus on what can I do, what can I see? How can I upgrade my knowledge? How can I upgrade my skills? How can I shift and adapt?

John Assaraf:

In this pandemic the number one skill I am training all of my clients on, ready? It's called becoming an adaptationist. Adaptationist. When I was in the Galapagos Island, and Raymond and I talked a couple weeks ago, he was there as well, when I was in the . . . He wasn't with me. He was on a different trip. When I was in the Galapagos Island, I was following Darwin's trail, the one that he did on the beagle, and I was reading his autobiography and I found this hat that says Evolve or Become Extinct. Evolve or become extinct. Well let me share something with you. In every recession or downturn in the market that I've been in, I think this is the fifth one since 1980, there are people who got healthier. There are people who made millions and billions. There are people who started companies including Pinterest and Airbnb and numerous others. There are people that took their imagination and focused it on the positive, on adaptation, on innovation, on how can I, on what is needed right now? Everything is changing in cities, in apartments, in what we're going to need for our health, digital services. The question is how can you be a part of that if you're focusing on all of the negative disempowering parts of this and how it's affecting you and how you don't like it and how it's disrupting your comfort zone? Guess what? You can't be focusing on the opportunities.

John Assaraf:

Why? Because our brain tends to mono focus on whatever we give energy or attention. The key here is to learn how can I be aware of when my Frankenstein brain is active and how can I deliberately choose to activate my Einstein part of the brain? Does that sound awesome? Here's what happens. When the stress circuit is activated the motivational circuit is actually shut off. When the stress circuit is activated a lot of the blood flow is going to a part of your brain that wants you to be prepared to either just shut down, freeze, to run away, flee, or to do what? To fight it. Guess what? If you're fighting against yourself you are disempowering yourself. But if you're focusing on what can I do, what are the possibilities, what is here for me to learn, what is here for me to upgrade, now you're activating the motivational circuit which is the nucleus accumbent and insula part of the brain. Now your releasing dopamine, and if you release dopamine, the feel-good neurochemical, you've just opened up the channel to the Einstein brain and you've opened up the channel to acting and behaving in ways that are aligned with what it is you want versus what you don't want.

John Assaraf:

Here's how you do it. I wrote a book called Innercise. It's a bestselling book, and one of the first things that I teach in the book is innercise number one, it's called Take 6 - Calm the Circuits. Now if you think for just a moment about your brain. All right, forget about your face, your features, your hair, your eyes, your nose, forget about all that. If you go underneath one layer, what are you? You're a brain and a nervous system. You're a brain and a nervous system. Now the brain, or your brain, all right, has got a sympathetic nervous system and a parasympathetic nervous system. Sympathetic is our stress response reactive system that's automatic deep inside the deepest neural structures of your brain. Then we have the common response circuit, the parasympathetic nervous system.

John Assaraf:

In a state of stress, anxiety, fear, worry, uncertainty, we can see that blood flow and that circuit activated. The easiest, simplest way in the world for you to just manage those two systems, sympathetic or parasympathetic, is if you take six deep breaths. Maybe you want to do it with me. Put a hand, okay, on your belly button. Just put one hand gently on your belly button and one hand so you can feel your lungs expand, so maybe just in the middle of your chest. If you take a very, very, very slow deep breath in through your nose slowly, like six seconds, seven seconds, and make sure that your hand over your belly button rises first. Instead of feeling your lungs first, make the air go into your diaphragm first and then your lungs and then hold it for two seconds. Then as you blow it out slowly, slowly, slowly in six second increments, blow out like you're blowing out through a straw. One more time. Hold it at the top for two or three seconds.

John Assaraf:

Now here's what we know. If you took six deep breaths that slowly in through your nose and out through your mouth like you're blowing out through a straw, you deactivate the fear, the worry, the stress, the uncertainty circuits in your brain and you then activate the Einstein part of your brain. I'll show you what to do with that in just a moment.

John Assaraf:

Let's go back to this first innercise, Take 6 - Calm the Circuits. You can also do a mini advanced version of this where you breathe in and all you have to do is go, "I breathe in calmness. I breathe out stress, worry, fear, uncertainty." You could breathe in anything and breathe out anything.

John Assaraf:

Now why does that work? The answer is because any time you use a language pattern your brain understands what it is that you're breathing in or out and your thalamus actually releases the neurochemical that's associated with the word that you are using. If you are breathing in calmness, your brain knows what calmness is so it releases the neurochemical of calmness and your brain knows what the neurochemical of stress is so it releases that as well. Now you're giving an instruction to your brain.

John Assaraf:

Now if you just set up a bell on your computer or on your mobile phone where you had a bell go off once an hour and you did an innercise called Take 6 - Calm the Circuits, and then right after that 60, 70 seconds you did the second innercise called AIA, A-I-A. AIA stands for awareness, intention, action. Now ones that you want to be aware of. The first thing that you want to be aware of in a calm, relaxed, activated Einstein brain is what have I been thinking for the last hour? What have I been feeling for the last hour? It's awareness of thoughts, emotions, feelings, sensations, and behaviors. What have I been doing for the last hour?

John Assaraf:

> Now remember this. Awareness is what gives you choice and choice is what actually gives you freedom. If you want to have more choice, become more aware. In this aware state, relaxed, calm aware state, now I can say, "Well I'm aware that I've been talking negatively," or "I'm aware that I'm feeling a little bit off," or "I'm aware that I've been wasting a lot of time this last hour." Well guess what? Then you go to the I, intention. Well great, and by the way, when you do the AIA innercise, you must do it without judgment, blame, shame, guilt or justification. Let me repeat. Without any judgment, blame, shame, guilt or justification. Just pure awareness of the processes that are going on in your brain, in your heart, in your gut, and in your behavior.

John Assaraf:

> Then in that state of awareness you can say okay, my intention for the next hour is to be calm, to be happy, to be focused, to be highly productive. That's my intention. Awesome. Then you go, "Okay, what's one little small action step I could do right now?" Not in an hour, not in two or three, right now, right following the AIA innercise you take one positive action.

> Why do you do that? Well you do that because now you're retraining your brain to be in a state of awareness, to be in a state of intentionality, and to be in a state of positive constructive actions that'll move you towards your goals instead of away from them. Now you are using your brain instead of allowing your brain to be using you. Now who's in control? Now who's running the show? Now who has more personal power? Your old habits, or the new ones that you are creating?

John Assaraf:

Is this making sense so far? Raymond, I've got four minutes left on my clock over here. Let's go to Flip the Switch. Now let me show you something.

Raymond Aaron:

Go for it. You're doing great.

John Assaraf:

Let me just show you something. I can't believe that all of you are just over here wasting time. Oh my God, I'm so sad today. I can't believe what's going on. Now what did I just do? There's some stuff that you learn if you've ever done any acting or stage work, and if you've ever been part of an actor's studio. It's called flip the switch.

John Assaraf:

Now we all have emotions and for most people emotions control their behavior. Well if you're a Hollywood actor, imagine if you're even not a Hollywood actor right now and somebody tapped you on the shoulder and it was your favorite Hollywood actor or actress and he or she said to you, "Hey, we just finished writing this script and we think you'd be perfect for this script. Would you consider reading the script for us? It's got some parts of it where you're angry, where you're playing the victim, where you're unhappy, where you're sad, where you're super happy, you feel mega successful. All of this is in this script. Could you practice this just for one minute to see if you even make a possible candidate for this movie? And if we choose you, we'll pay you a million bucks." How many of you could pretend you're happy or pretend you're sad or pretend you're mad or pretend you're guilty or pretend any of the emotions that you would need if a Hollywood actor offered you a million dollars to play a role? The answer is, almost every human being could either play the role right now or learn how to.

John Assaraf:

What does that tell you? It tells you that you are not a victim of your emotions. You just haven't learned how to control them and activate them. You haven't yet learned how to be aware of and change your mental and emotional state because you haven't practiced.

John Assaraf:

When we learn that we can control our state, we can control what we can focus on, we can control and get better at managing our emotions so we are empowered, focused, we feel good, we're alive, we're focusing on how we can and why we can versus why we can't or why we won't. When you start to learn some of these little innercises and you practice them either on your own or guided, now you start to use your bio-computer the way it was meant to be used with you controlling it versus it controlling you. Now you're in the driver's seat. Now you can take a vision, you can set goals, and now you can direct yourself to achieving every one of your goals and dreams regardless of the pandemic and because of the pandemic you could be one of the 2% or 3% that thrives instead of survives or goes backwards.

John Assaraf:

Raymond, I'm done. I've got one-minute left on my clock.

Raymond Aaron:

You're amazing. I love it. You got me right at the beginning with the word innercise instead of exercise. From then on, I was in love with you. It's incredible.

John Assaraf:

Thank you.

Raymond Aaron:

What a title of a book. Oh my gosh. I wish you the best of success. Sell millions of copies.

John Assaraf:

Thank you, my friend.

Raymond Aaron:

You led off the entire day two because I knew you would set the stage of positivity and insights, and you did a brilliant job. Thank you so, so much.

John Assaraf:

Thank you, my friend. I just want to congratulate everybody that's here upgrading their knowledge, their skills, their mindset, their awareness, because you are the ones that are going to make the difference in this new world right now. Thank you, Raymond. Thanks everyone.

Raymond Aaron:

Thank you. Great to see you again.

John Assaraf:

Bye everyone.

Raymond Aaron:

Bye-bye.

Your Office Can Help Manifest Your Prosperity Especially During Isolation

Marie Diamond

Raymond Aaron:

You are so special to me. First of all, I'd like everyone to know Marie diamond is my wife's coach. Marie Diamond was the star of the Secret. Marie Diamond is one of the top unbelievable grand masters, huge Poo bah of a Feng shui. And she is a true master. And I'm so excited that you're on. So this is now two in a row stars from the Secret John Assaraf was on right before you. And I also have some [inaudible 00:00:33] today, which you don't know. Of the speakers who shared in order to help promote World Prosper Summit, you're the number one, thank you. You shared more than any other speaker. Now there's a big contest for who can share more, but the speakers and my staff are not eligible. So I'm just giving you a thank you, not a prize. But I love you and, and go, you got half an hour because then I've got someone else right after you. I love you. Dazzle my listeners.

Marie Diamond:

Okay, wonderful. So thank you so much for sharing and doing this wonderful experience for all the people out there. So happy with that. So I hope you can see my screen. This is the first time I'm using this.

Raymond Aaron:

Yes we can [crosstalk 00:01:29] yes.

Marie Diamond:

Perfect. Okay, lovely. So what I, first of all would like to talk about is a little bit to introducing myself. I know some of you don't know me very well. Perhaps you have seen me in the Secret. So I'm the only European teacher in the Secret actually. And I'm a lawyer from background and the criminologist. And I started working in that field in Belgium. I'm originally from there. And as a teaching about meditation and Feng shui 25 years ago. And I became one of the teachers in the Secret. And I attracted that completely in, by using the work I'm going to share with you.

Marie Diamond:

I live now between London and the South of France with my husband and my children. I'm like Raymond I'm part of the Transformation Leadership Council. And I founded the association of transformational leaders in Europe. And we have online more than 2 million students on Feng shui on Dao Zhang, and on meditation. And so these are a few of my clients, Jack Canfield, Bob Proctor, Rhonda Byrne, and then some of my major clients like Steven Spielberg and Rolling Stones. So there are some of my clients.

Marie Diamond:

But what I really, really want to talk to you about is about the law of attraction and perhaps an aspect of the law of attraction that you have probably not really heard of. And when I started studying Feng shui, and the law of attraction and meditation, I connected with the grand master of Feng shui. And he told me that there are actually three aspects of the law of attraction. And that completed within my view on the law of attraction. I had done meditation since I was seven years old and I connected with my soul. And I knew that connecting with my spirit with a higher source than my personality did created a lot of attraction for me, that was different than other people. Because their focus and their energy is towards what they do to their ego surviving, and not having a purpose and living a purpose with their soul.

Marie Diamond:

And so I understood that all the people that are focusing on spirituality, connecting in religion, that they are actually activating what we call the heavenly part of the law of attraction. That's why I do believe in meditation. I do believe in prayer. Because it brings you in connection with something completely different. It's not your ego, it's not your body, it's not your mind. It is the life force, the spirit that lives through you and in you. And so the law of attraction is able to work on that level. Because when you do prayers and affirmations and meditations, you actually are activating the law of attraction on that level.

Marie Diamond:

Now, some people would call that your karma, your destiny, but I would say it really is not completely directing you. Some people would say, well, everything is my karma, but actually that is not true. According to Feng shui, it's only 33% that your life, turns out a certain way because of what you attracted as a soul to go through in this lifetime. And interesting enough, if you have a talent, if you have a skill set and you're born with, this is part of your heavenly luck. Perhaps also some challenges that you have since you are born, that are part of perhaps some of your destiny to learn from all of this.

Marie Diamond:

Now, second part of the law of attraction, according to Feng shui is your human luck. That means how is your thinking? How do you feel? What actions do you take? And you just heard, I'm sure a wonderful explanation from John around the thoughts and the mind and how you can switch that around and even on the feelings level. So this is actually where the self help and self development is really focused on. And that's in the Secret, of course. We are focusing very much on the human luck, how you are as a human being, with the talents and the gifts that you have received from your soul. How do you express that?

Marie Diamond:

Now we also see that this is about one third of your outcome. So it's not a hundred percent. That's why a lot of people think the Secret doesn't always work for them. Because they're thinking if I think positive, if I feel positive and in gratitude, and I take massive action that I ultimately will manifest everything. And fung shui masters are saying, this is only one third of your results of the law of attraction. So it's not a hundred percent.

Marie Diamond:

And there is another part of the law of attraction called the earth luck, your environment. And this is actually, I remember when

I connected with Rhonda Byrne and the Secret that I started sharing that because the secret wasn't very much working. It was not moving forward. There were no people that were really interested in buying the DVD. And so I came in and started working with earth luck. And so I did, I call it my magic, using Feng shui and Dao Zhang to change her office. I did that also for about 50% of the teachers in the Secret, and the publisher, and the PR agent.

Marie Diamond:

And so I actually used the law of attraction of the environment of where you live and your home. And especially in this difficult time where you literally need to be at home and be trying to create a prosperity where you live as much as you can and doing online work and online promotions. This is actually super important because your home is your first place of living, of being. Because you don't probably go to your job. You don't go to your office. So everything goes on into your home.

And so according to Feng shui masters, that's also responsible for one third, 33.3%, of the results of the law of attraction. And I really want to teach you this time in how to create that. Some very practical tips that I'm going to go and lead you through to really get all of this.

Marie Diamond:

So I want you to start thinking about your home is a vision board. You know, in the Secret John was explaining, John Assaraf, about the vision board and I know many of you probably have a vision board. And what is a vision board? It's a two-dimensional piece of paper where you put pictures and images on and your dreams and you express them so that they're not just in your mind, but they're like something physically to see visual you have, that you can connect with.

Marie Diamond:

And so what I learned from Feng shui as a Feng shui master is that everything around you is actually acting as a vision board. So all that is around you is literally creating a reality in your subconscious mind. And so perhaps you have images, colors, furniture, statues, and it's all plays somewhere. They'll the way you are surrounding yourself with this is influencing you 24 hours a day. Constantly gives you vibrations energy to your subconscious mind.

Marie Diamond:

And so sometimes people are like, yes, I'm ready for change. And then instead of changing their mind and start changing their environment, they are painting, they buy new furniture, they're buying like new lights. So they are feeling that they have to change something in the outside world. And so there's two ways to change. It's like I go from within me. Or I go from the outside to within me.

And so, one of the things I've learned is that a lot of people are stuck in the law of attraction because what happens is their last part of the law of attraction is not aligned in harmony with the thoughts, the feelings and the actions they are creating. And is not in alignment with their destiny and the purpose they have in this life.

Marie Diamond:

So I'm going to give you a few tips here to really immediately start looking differently into your house. So the three places that influence you the most for prosperity and for relationships is actually first of all, your living area. So where you are spending, most of the people spend three to five hours a day, in their living space, watching television, being with their family. And right now, in these difficult times, some of you are spending there probably 10 to 12 hours a day. So everything that is there is influencing you constantly on a very subconscious level.

And the living room is affecting you both for your success, your prosperity health relationship, and motivation. Now your bedroom, it's also influencing you and it influences you of course, first. So your romantic relationships, so where you sleep, the things that are surrounding yourself and that alone is a whole class. If you want to attract more romance to focus on that. Also the bedroom creates money. But a lot of people are not even aware of because when the morning comes and you wake up and you have good energy, then you have had a good sleep. You had a wonderful, harmonious night, you have more ability to create prosperity. You have new ideas, you have new energy to tackle the day.

Marie Diamond:

And of course your office, your workspace, and for some of you right now, that's perhaps that's your dining room or that's in a space in your home. Or this just sitting in your couch, a place where you work online or you are connecting with the world from this lock down situation into the world. And so it does influence your money, your prosperity, success, and professional relationships. So what can we do to really go there?

Marie Diamond:

And I'm sure some of you are like now thinking, "Oh my God, I'm in a huge mess, a huge struggle because my office and my bedroom and my living room, it is quite a mess." And so indeed, one of the things I have understood over these years is that yeah, also order creates a different vibration than chaos. And so when you have your home full of clutter, full of chaos, things are not put in the right place. Your brainwaves will actually connect in with that subconsciously with that order, with that chaos and that clutter, and it will have more lower beta brainwaves. And it's harder to concentrate, it's harder to focus, it's harder to even come up with new ideas around prosperity. It's even harder to focus on your job or on what you are accomplishing in your business.

Marie Diamond:

So if you have the left picture and it looks like this with a lot of things laying around, then it is really time. And perhaps now in this lock down situation and these difficult times, it's possible a perfect time to say like, "Well, let me clear up a little bit. Let me create space." We have now the time, but now let's create space. And when you create space and order and you declutter, you actually create abundance. How many times I went through my closet and I found, cash money. Recently, I went through a closet and I found an envelope with a thousand dollars. I'm like, where did I come from? Somewhere I tucked it away. Some money I even forgot about. Or you find a business card of somebody you're thinking, wow, that would be an amazing connection.

Marie Diamond:

Or it could be, a file that you put away and you think, Oh, that was a great idea, but you never did something with it. Or a book that is the perfect time to read right now. So as you are creating order and you declutter, you are creating alpha brainwaves. So you come from a beta house or beta space into an alpha space. In the alpha space, you will be focused and you will have insights, you'll have more creativity, you will feel more uplifted. So change your home just by decluttering. That's the first part of your, I would say, journey I would invite you to take right now. And to change your brain energy and your feelings about living in your space. And I'm telling you, you will find treasures and you will totally see that as amazing things fill in your home that you haven't even paid attention to.

Marie Diamond:

So think always about you are like the king and the queen, a president in your home. And so think about your home as a castle, as a temple, as something that is a sacred space for you. A sacred space for you to create prosperity. And so if you think about the king or queen, or a president, I'm sure their castle, their palace is squeaky clean. So you can say, "Well, they have people to help," but you know, you need to, at the beginning, do it yourself and make it orderly so that there's space for prosperity to come into your life.

Marie Diamond:

The second tip I want to give you is how you set yourself up in your environment and you see here an image and it's called a poverty position. So when you have a desk that is facing the wall, then you're actually literally telling to your energy field, "I will hit a wall." I will not see perspective. Because if you see the wall, there is no horizon, there's no focus. You literally are going to get stuck somewhere because your focus gets stuck. Even if you have the computer in front of you, when you are sitting in such a position that you're facing the wall, most of the time, you will not see the door.

And so when you don't see the door, you actually are in a position where you have no ability to see who can come in. Even if you work at home, who comes into the door, is your client, it is your family, it is the income streams. Income streams do not come in through walls. They don't come in through windows, even if you put your desk in front of a window, it's the same situation.

Marie Diamond:

I remember many years ago, when I went to the home and the office of Jack Canfield, he was sitting with his back to the door, overlooking an amazing view. And I said, Jack, money doesn't come through the window. Money always comes with people through the door. So we changed that around. And so all the things were that were stuck for him, started really flowing back into his life. So imagine that the door is the income energy. That is where the prosperity can come in. People that come through the walls or come through the windows, they are the ones taking your money. Also, when you're facing a wall, you are in what we call a beta position. Again, you'll be more stressed, less focused. So try for sure to change that around and get yourself into a abundance position.

So an abundance position means that your desk is facing the door. Now, as you're working probably at home, it could be sitting in your dining room that you're always making sure when you're working, you see the door when you're setting in your couch, your sofa see the door, when you're in your bedroom, make sure when you wake up, you see the door. So the more you see the door, the more your brain opens up. You see a horizon, you see space, you see possibilities in front of you. You are not hitting the wall. You are seeing the potential in front of you, the full potential.

Marie Diamond:

And so your brainwaves actually will go into alpha brain waves. When that happens, you will be more calmer, more focused, more creative. So you can imagine, if you think about the CEO of any big company, they're never sitting with their back to the door and facing the wall. They will always have a back supporting them, like it could be a high back chair, could be a wall, something supporting them. And you have space in front of them to talk to someone. Because when you are sitting in such a way that you're focusing towards the wall, you have not even a communication. Nobody can sit on the other side. There's no space for clients.

Marie Diamond:

So the next step is that after decluttering and connecting in, and positioning yourself in the right way, is that everyone has a success direction. And so in order to find out your success direction, I invite you to go to Mariediamond.com and to get your free energy report. And in there, you will have to put in your gender, your birthday and you will get an 18-page report to start the law of attraction in your office, in your home. And you will ask you to find out that you have a success direction.

Marie Diamond:

And so what is a success of action? Well, there are eight compass directions. And so, one of these compass directions is based on your birthday. It gives you a success area. Mine is Southwest. So Southwest is where I then put in my office, in my bedroom, in my living room. I pay attention, what do I place there? So think about your office, your living room, your bedroom. It is a small vision board for prosperity. So what you do is you always stand in the center of that space and then you take a compass and you can actually then see where in that space is the compass direction that you have a success.

Marie Diamond:

And then first of all, you are going to declutter that area. You always make sure that in that success direction, there is, no shoes, no boxes, no wastebasket, no paper shredder. I've seen it all. Because everything that is there has been influencing your prosperity. As long as you've been living in that space, if you've been sleeping, working or living there.

So what you can do to also make it easier to get your success direction. I have a free app, a Marie Diamond app. And in there, again, you can click on your gender, put in your birthday, and then you get actually this compass that you see, and there is a success direction. And you can then use that as a compass. So you don't have to buy a compass. You just go and get a free download of the app. And it actually will show you in your space, where is your success direction.

Marie Diamond:

And so in that success direction, after you have decluttered it, you also have to activate your success direction with the right items, the right statues, the right images. So what you can do, if you have a business, you can put there your business cards, perhaps you have a vision board. That's a perfect place to put in your success direction. Perhaps you have awards and certificates, products that you have created, flyers. If you don't have any of that, I'm sure you have some amazing books from the wonderful teachers that are part of the World Prosper Summit.

Marie Diamond:

So you can put there some books of very successful people, books on prosperity. Because then you actually start influencing and creating a three-dimensional vision board. And this way you will actually start enhancing your office, your bedroom, your living room, with 33.3%. And it will be very interesting for you to see when you look at your success direction and you have placed there something, what that actually is about.

Marie Diamond:

I was recently in somebody's home of a very, very successful television coach on body and exercise. And he said to me like, "You know, I feel like there's no new things coming to me. Like, it's all the same old, same old." And I said to him, "Well, if I look at your success direction . . ." He had put some books from the past and some programs, but he also had put some very old ceramics, like broken ceramics there. I said, "Yeah, I like that kind of thing. But what are you telling? What is the message you're giving yourself? Are you in the ceramic business? Are you in the antique business?" He said "No, I am into the body business." I said, "Okay, well, get some awards, get some of your amazing books and programs and put them in there." And I said, "What was the most successful program you ever had to do? Well, there was a program that I did in the early nineties," And I said, "Okay, put it there. That's the most successful."

Marie Diamond:

And so a week later, a television program, a television channel called him and said, "We heard of you that in the nineties, you did this amazing program to do exercise from your chair. And we would invite you to start doing this now in this lock down time. Could you do some programs for that?" And so now he's all over the internet with his old program in a new little story, in a new little way of bringing it online. And he's like, "Oh my God, I put it there, and a week later." And it's really interesting what you will see when you change your environment. It takes about nine days, nine weeks, to feel the shift that is happening.

So I'm inviting you to try this out. And then one small thing for prosperity for 2020 . . . So every year there is some cashflow energy and this year the cash flow prosperity is very strong in the Northeast and the Southeast section of an office or a living room. So declutter, the Northeast and the Southeast section. And if you want to attract more cashflow or new income streams, you can put there a bubbling fountain, just a nice bubbling fountain. If you cannot do that, place some gold items, some gold symbols in that area.

Marie Diamond:

So this is what I wanted to share with you to really get into this information. And I hope this was helpful for all of you.

Raymond Aaron:

Marie. Oh, where did she go? Yes.

Marie Diamond:

I am here. I'm here. I just don't know how I have to get back onto my screen.

Raymond Aaron:

The little camera button. Just click the camera button.

Marie Diamond:

Okay. Okay. Here we go, yes.

Raymond Aaron:

It worked. I want you to know that I face this gorgeous, beautiful eight-foot-tall Buddha. It's just so beautiful. On the other hand, it's a damn wall. And when I look at the Southeast, it's where I store my luggage for going on trips and there's no trips anymore. When I look at the Southeast . . . . That's the Northeast. When I look at the Southeast, it's an old bookshelf where I just throw crap. Oh my God, I've got to clean up.

Marie Diamond:

So you better clean up for sure.

Raymond Aaron:

If look way over here, I can just barely see my door. I've got to completely rearrange. Now, I am very clean and orderly and decluttered. Really, really, really. But the only two places that are bad are the Northeast and the Southeast. Oh my God. I'm so grateful to you. You're such a master.

Marie Diamond:

Thank you. And good luck for the rest of the day with the World Prosperity Summit.

Raymond Aaron:

Aren't you sweet and thank you. I want to remind you again, you were the number one sharer of all the speakers. You did a wonderful job for me. I'm so honored. My wife says hello to you, my wife loves you.

Marie Diamond:

Okay. Bye, bye.

Raymond Aaron:

Bye bye.

The 8 Laws of Money

Joe Vitale

Raymond Aaron:

The next speaker is Joe Vitale. Joe Vitale, just click on your video button, Joe. Let's see, Joe Vitale is here.

Joe Vitale:

I'm right here.

Raymond Aaron:

Yeah, there he is. Joe, you are the third in a row superstar from The Secret. We've had John Assaraf and Marie Diamond and you, three in a row. We thought we'd start day two, but the biggest possible bang. And I just acknowledge Marie Diamond for being the number one sharer amongst the speakers. But what I didn't tell her is that she was tied for number one, with you. [crosstalk 00:00:40] So congratulations, the two of you are my dearest friends, the other speakers, they shared a little bit, but not with their heart. And the two of you did. And so I'll love you forever.

Joe Vitale:

I already love you. So thank you for saying that though. I appreciate it.

Raymond Aaron:

So by way of very brief introduction, yes, he was the superstar of the movie The Secret. Yes, he is a musician. Yes, he's written over 50 books and he's happy and he's loving and he does everything with gusto and he's just, his heart is as big as a continent. I love him, Joe, you got half an hour. Take them . . . I just want to say one thing at 12:30 PM, eastern time, I'm going to announce the sharers, the top 20 sharers amongst the participants and the number one sharer gets a prize worth $10,000, US. Be happy, Joe.

Joe Vitale:

All right. Be happy and expect miracles. That's what's behind me here. Thank you, Raymond. And I want everybody to give him a standing ovation. I know there's people all over the planet that are tuning in to this right now. And I just wanted to acknowledge him. He put this together himself. He invited everybody himself. He did this out of the goodness of his heart and all the people who have come in have all agreed to do it for nothing. They all waived their fees were all showing up at whatever odd times they are for all of us around the planet. Raymond, thank you. I love you. And I love what you've done here. So thank you. So I'm going to take my 30 minutes and run. So get out of here.

First of all, I want to acknowledge that we're in something called a pandemic and I've been making videos to tell people that there's actually two viruses going on. And this is important to my topic. My topic is the Eight Laws of Money. But before

I tell you what those eight laws are, I want to remind you that there are actually two viruses going on right now. The very first virus is the virus that everybody knows about and everybody's talking about and the news won't shut up about. That virus is when we want to be on alert about and to take care of our health for, so do whatever the health authorities are telling you to do, wash your hands, do social distancing, blah, blah, blah. I'm not dismissing it at all. It is real, and we want to take care of ourselves. But the second virus is worse than the first. The second virus is a virus of the mind. And the virus of the mind is fear. When we fall into fear, not only does life look pretty bad and we feel pretty bad, but ironically, we lower our immune system.

Joe Vitale:

When we lower our immune system, guess what? That first virus has an opportunity to come visit. So what I want to encourage everybody to do is to drop the fear and move to faith. I'm not, again, dismissing anything that's going on in terms of a virus. But I am saying that we need to fortify ourselves mentally with positive thinking. I do have a sign behind me that says be happy. I do have another side that says, expect miracles. I'm also wearing an expect miracle shirts. All of these are my somewhat subtle attempts to get us to move in a new direction. Jason Mraz has a new song right now called *Look For The Good* and I love the song and I love the concept. I recorded a song a while back called *Look For The Light*. And this goes all the way back to the Glad Game with Pollyanna in 1913, saying play the Glad Game. There's always something good to find and something good to focus on.

Joe Vitale:

So my invitation to you is to focus on the good, to focus on the happy, to focus on what's working, to focus on what you are grateful for. Gratitude is the single most powerful thing you can do to change your life and you can do it right now. Now, everybody watching this is already moving in the right direction because you're here. Raymond gathered the crowd, Raymond gathered the speakers and everybody is here and what we're giving you is positivity. So I want you to soak it up and I want you to implement it. This is not a onetime experience where you just feel this and then you go back to bed or turn on Netflix again, this is something that you want to integrate and then utilize and implement. So with that said, what I'm talking about is the Eight Laws of Money.

Joe Vitale:

And I've heard people say "Money, can't bring happiness." And I've also heard people say, "You don't know where to shop." I've also heard people say "Poverty, doesn't bring happiness either." So what you want is a healthy relationship with money, especially right now. I actually regard right now as a good thing. We've all been sent to our room, so to speak. And we've been put on a spiritual retreat. This is our opportunity to go inside ourselves, not inside our houses or just inside our houses, but inside ourselves. And we can meditate, we can reflect, we can reset, we can create, we can do a lot of things inside ourselves. And it's all beginning with a new mindset. And the mindset I want to talk about is around money.

Joe Vitale:

Now I have a new book, that shouldn't surprise anybody who knows me. In fact, I have two new books, but I'm not going to go crazy here. Money Loves Speed. And what I'm going to read, this has the Eight Laws of Money in it. Money Loves Speed: From Stress to Success: Revealing the 8 Laws of Money Fast. I'm not holding it up because I'm trying to get you to buy it. You can go to the library and get it. But the Eight Laws are in this book and I want to take them one at a time and explain them to you. So this is going to be a read and riff experience, which I've never done before. And I've never done it live with thousands of people all over the world, watching me stumble my way through this.

Joe Vitale:

So the Eight Laws of Money, the very first law, money loves freedom. Money loves freedom. So let me read the paragraph about it. And then I'll riff on it. Money doesn't have any beliefs about you. You have beliefs about money. Those beliefs create a mindset and money will always match your mindset. You don't see reality, you see your version of reality. As Arnold Patent said, "We don't create abundance, we create limitations." Money loves the freedom of an unlimited mind. Release your blocks and money will be free to come to you. Money loves freedom.

Joe Vitale:

So that's a paragraph from the book, Money Loves Speed, which we're going to get to in a second. Money loves freedom is referring to your mindset. As I've often said, that money matches your mindset. If you have negative beliefs about money, if you have negative beliefs about yourself, if you have limiting beliefs about deservingness, if you have limiting beliefs about opportunity and possibility, you will limit money and its ability to get to you. Money loves freedom means you need to wide open the space here in your brain so that you can see the opportunities and act on the opportunities and profit from the opportunities without interference.

Joe Vitale:

I love Arnold Patents quote when he said that we don't create abundance, we create limitations. Think about that. We create the limitations. When we look out into the world and we think there's no opportunities or there's few opportunities, where we've lost our job or were laid off because of what's going on with the pandemic, at this point, we fall into fear. Those closed off feelings and those perceived limitations are not coming from reality, I know you can argue for that, but they're coming from your perception of reality. Surely you know that there are people making money right now. Surely you know that are people creating new products and services right now. Surely you know that there are people who are looking at the idea that they are stuck at home as an opportunity to become an entrepreneur. Surely you know there are people who are looking at the very same thing you're looking at, but because they have a freedom and an openness in their mind, they're seeing what you may not be seeing. Money loves freedom. So what you have to do there is find the limiting beliefs and remove eliminate beliefs.

Joe Vitale:

And let me go through these other laws to see if it helps make all of this clearer for you. So the very first law in the book Money Loves Speed is money loves freedom. The second law is the title itself, money loves speed. So I'm going to read the paragraph from the book. Act on your ideas and ride the energy of the moment. The faster you move when an idea occurs to you, the more you can see the energy of the idea to manifest it. Plus, the faster you act, the faster you get your idea to marketplace.

Usually the first person to the table wins. An idea has energy. When you quickly act on it, you get to leverage that energy to manifest your idea. So don't dilly dally, second guess or delay, money loves speed.

Joe Vitale:

All right, so let me riff on that for a second. Raymond introduced me by saying I've written 50 books. He doesn't know that I've written 80 books. 80 books and not only I said, this is the most reason book Money Loves Speed. It's not. I came out with a book right after it called The Art and Science of Results. How did I do this? Because money loves speed. That's how I'm able to do this. When an idea comes to me, I've already created the space for opportunity because money loves freedom. The first law.

Joe Vitale:

So the second law with money loves speed means the faster I act on that idea, the faster I get it done and the faster I get it to marketplace. So I don't have blocks in my brain saying, "I can't write a book or nobody's going to be interested in the book." That's all gone because of the first law, so I implement the second law and before you know it, the book's done. Raymond mentioned I'm a musician. I have 15 albums. Some of the people that are professional musicians that have been doing this for six decades, don't have 15 albums. I have 15 albums in about six years. Why? Because money loves speed. When an idea comes to me, I act on it and act as quickly as I can.

Joe Vitale:

I'm aware of the times flying through here, talk about speed. So let me go to law number three, money loves to be appreciated. This single law, this single law can transform your relationship to money right now. Money loves to be appreciated. Let me quickly read the paragraph from the book. Arnold Patent, one of my heroes, he said "The sole purpose of money is to express appreciation." Think about that. "The sole purpose of money is to express appreciation." You don't spend, unless it's for something you want or need, appreciate what you are buying and you will transform your relationship to money. Instead of grumbling about a lack of money, focus on the money you do have and as you spend save or invest it, focus on appreciating the fact that you are getting something in return for your money. Money loves appreciation.

Joe Vitale:

I can riff on that one line for an, I was going to say an hour but week, for a week. In fact, it's the opening line in my book, I dedicated the book to Arnold Patent's insight, the sole purpose of money is to express appreciation. Think about this. When you write a check for your phone bill, aren't you grateful to have a phone? When you write a check for your mortgage, aren't you grateful to have your apartment or your condo or your house or wherever you live? When you write a check for your groceries, aren't you grateful to have food? See, most people are grumbling and complaining and they're not grateful. But if you move into a new awareness and a new relationship with money, you can start to befriend money and money will come to you because money needs appreciated. Money loves to be appreciated was number three.

Joe Vitale:

Number four, money loves attention. I gave a seminar decades ago and Dee Wallace, a famous actress, was one of my speakers. Absolutely loved her and her presentation was unforgettable. And she said, "What's the best relationship you've ever had. Best sharing, talking, loving, lusting." And then she said, "Do you have that relationship with money?" It hit me because I realized, myself at the time, and everybody else, we don't have a relationship with money except a bitter complaining one. It's more of a love, hate relationship. It's not one of appreciation. So the eight laws of money and money, number four, law number four is money, loves attention. Most people don't pay any attention to money except to complain about the lack of it. What if you had a more loving and grateful relationship with it? Instead of regarding money as impersonal in inanimate, what have you thought of it as a feeling energy? What if you pretended it was a life force instead of acting as if money was nothing, act as if money was everything, as important as a family member or pet. Money loves attention.

Joe Vitale:

All right. Because I'm on number four and I'm running out of time or at least it's moving very quickly. I want to go to law number five, money loves energy. Money loves energy. Have you ever thought about any of these laws before? Are they new to you? Because they've been new to me. I was homeless at one point, I was in poverty for 10 years. I didn't know all of these laws. These are the kinds of things that have changed my life forever. And I'm trying to give you a condensed version of the laws. The rest of it is all in the book, of course, Money Loves Speed. And I'll tell you how to get it for $2 later.

Joe Vitale:

But money loves energy. At the same event I gave years ago, Bill Phillips, the *Body For Life* fitness legend was one of the speakers. I love Bill, he changed my life. I was in his Body For life Program back in 2005, probably nine times. And I got honorable mentions out of it. And I went in his transformation camp several years ago, four times, and I have a metal from it. So he's deeply influenced me. And one of the things he teaches and I learned is that the healthier you are, the wealthier you can be. I'm going to repeat it, this is from Bill Phillips. The healthier you are, the wealthier you can be. Money requires energy to circulate and appreciate, enjoy money and be healthy enough to circulate it. The better you feel about yourself, the more you will feel deserving of good things, such as money. Being healthy allows you to have more energy and use more energy. You will then have the stamina to be a wise pilot for money. Money loves energy.

Joe Vitale:

These are fantastic insights. Let me give you law number six, money loves to circulate. Money loves to circulate. Prosperous purchasing, when the desire is there and the money is there you must spend it to send a signal of abundance to yourself. Not buying when you have the desire and the funds sends a signal of lack. Buying sends a signal of prosperity. Which do you want to reinforce? Also, giving money helps circulate it and creates a force to bring it back to you, multiplied. Just give where you receive spiritual nourishment and inspiration and not where you feel obligated to give. Money, loves to circulate.

Joe Vitale:

Well that's law number six. And again, like so many other laws, I can be talking about this for an entire week or more. These are very important. So let's look at two things about that particular law. One is I mentioned giving. Giving is one of the best ways to attract more money. If you're struggling with money right now, the best way to attract more is to give more. But I specify how to give. I say, ask yourself, where have you received spiritual or inspiration in the last week or so? Who spiritually nourished you or who inspired you? Could have been an Uber driver. It could have been an Amazon drop-off person that's delivering you your packages. It could be anybody, any place, any business, any organization. It can be anything. Wherever you were inspired. That's where you give 10% of your income and you do this on a regular basis and you do this without reservation, without expectation. You do not expect money to come back from whoever you gave it to.

Joe Vitale:

You expect it to come back from the cosmos, from the great something, from the universe, from God, from the divine. But you give. Most people will say, well, I can't give money, so I gave blood or I helped somebody. No, that's not giving, that's not tithing. That's not the principal I'm talking about. You have to give money and give it where you receive spiritual nourishment. That's the first level of the circulation. The second level is buying things. I call it prosperous purchasing. I said, I was going to tell you that for $2, you can have this book. For $2 you can have the audio of the book read by me and you can have the ebook of this. The book itself is on Amazon. But for only $2, you can have the ebook and the audio of this.

Joe Vitale:

Now, if you have $2 and you want this, you need to get it. You almost have to get it, because I call it prosperous purchasing. If you do the opposite, if you have $2 and you don't buy it, what have you told yourself? You're telling yourself, you live in lack, you live in limitation, that you don't deserve it. You're reinforcing negativity. Your money needs freedom, remember law, number one. And if you're not coming from that freedom, you're closing down the road to abundance to you. Again, I'm aware of time, so I'm talking fast.

Joe Vitale:

All right, so that was number six. Number seven, money loves respect. Money loves respect. Money is the root of all evil is a lie. Money is a tool to facilitate your dreams, respect money. It is a tool to fulfill dreams and a force for good in the world. Money is like a hammer or saw or any tool, respect it for what it can help you accomplish. Thinking money is somehow bad will push money away from you. Who wants anything bad in their life. Money loves respect. This seventh law is another biggie that I can talk quite a bit about, but let me see if I can help you. Because again, if you take this one in and integrate it and really hear what I'm saying, it can free you to have money.

Joe Vitale:

The phrase "Money is the root of all evil." Everybody's heard it. I've been in countries all over the world, Russia and Poland and Italy and Bermuda, and I don't know, every place around the planet. They all seem to share this belief that money is the root of all evil, but it's a belief. And it's an inaccurate belief. The phrase comes from a longer phrase in biblical literature. And I always remind people, we don't actually know what was said or written. We weren't there. And it was written in an archaic language, it was translated, retranslated, paraphrase, brought down to today and brought down with a lot of interpretation, misinterpretation and a lot of baggage. So the longer phrase is the "Love of money is the root of all evil." Which doesn't sound better. However, this is the big, however, I, and all the wealthy people I know that are balanced and healthy, do not love money.

Joe Vitale:

I do not love money. They appreciate it. Remember money loves appreciation. They appreciate it. They respect it. Money wants respect. They leverage it. They use it. It's a tool and only a tool. If I take, I have a pen around here someplace, a pen and said, pens are the root of all evil. A pen isn't a root of all evil. I might be able to stab somebody with this, and that would be a bad thing, but that would be me doing something bad, not the pen. Money in and of itself is fricking neutral. It is, in my opinion, a tool and a tool for good. That was number seven. Money loves respect.

Joe Vitale:

Number eight, money loves a mission. This is one of my favorites. Money loves a mission. Walt Disney said "We don't make movies to make money. We make money to make more movies." I love that. "We don't make movies to make money. We make money to make more movies." This is why I write books. I'm not selling these things to make money, I'm selling these things, so I make money so I can do more books. Books are my mission or more importantly, inspiring people through my books, through my music, through my speaking engagements, through the movies, through everything that I'm doing, is what's important to me. But if I make money from it, it enables me to keep doing it. Money loves mission. Be more focused on the end result than on the money to get to the end result. Focus on your life mission, not money. Dreams, attract funds. Missions, attract money. Be more focused on your life purpose and your life calling then on money. Money loves a mission.

Joe Vitale:

And this is where I would invite you to look within yourself and ask yourself what you think your contribution is to life itself. And don't dismiss yourself. Don't put yourself down, don't overlook your education, your background, your experience. I just re-read Viktor Frankl's famous book Man's Search For Meaning, and it was just an awe of such a amazing book and an amazing man and the times he went through. We think we went through tough times with a pandemic. My God, he was in a concentration camp. On a hundred years ago when there was the plague going around, we didn't have the Facebook, we didn't have social media, we didn't have the online world, which we take for granted sometimes. We live in a better time, an easier time, and what we're asked to do is something simple. Go to our room and stay healthy, stay safe and stay there. So while we're there, we get to reflect and we can ask our self, "What's my mission." And it doesn't have to be a mission that is so noble and so bold and so big that it just scares you and boggles your mind.

Joe Vitale:

It doesn't have to be curing cancer or curing the virus. If you've got a cure for cancer, please deliver it. Got a cure for the virus, please give it to us. But it could be like what I'm doing. I'm writing books. On one level, it's a small potatoes thing to do. So what? I'm an author, but that's important to me. Other people might need to be a great parent or maybe they're the boy scout or girl scout leader and they need to be the best at doing that and that's their sense of mission. Somebody else might have a mission to build schools in countries that are starving, or to bring water to countries that don't have it, or to bring vaccinations. There are so many different ways that you can contribute. I don't want to back anybody into a corner, but I want everybody to be thinking about it.

Joe Vitale:

You have a mission. Viktor Frankl in his book was saying, "Man search for meaning comes from man." You decide what your mission is. You are the one who give life meaning. So money loves a mission, but the mission comes from you. And during this time of a pandemic where we're being told, go inside and relax and reflect and meditate and contemplate, this is also our chance to connect to a sense of a mission. Whether it's making movies like Walt Disney did, or whether it's being an author for in my case or a singer in somebody else's case there, or any number of things, bake the best cookies. I don't know, it's going to be unique to you, but whatever it is for you pursue it like it's a mission. And that's really important because money loves a mission.

Joe Vitale:

So those are, my God, a super quick overview of the eight laws of money. They're from my book. Money Loves Speed. I said, you can have the book for $2. Go to Money Loves Speed book, moneylovesspeedbook.com, and you can have, for $2, the book audio read by me, and you can have the ebook so you can read along. If you want the actual printed book, you have to go to Amazon. And I don't know, I think it's $20 over there, but I've got a $2 offer for you. And remember what I said about prosperous purchasing, when an idea and an offer is in front of you and you have the money to buy it, assuming you have $2 US, and assuming that you want this, then you almost have to get it. You have to get it just to reinforce the idea of prosperity.

Joe Vitale:

And this book is full of other information. If you don't mind me just telling you, there are 35 ways to attract money, almost instantly. Also, right in the beginning if you're starving and you're almost homeless, believe me I know what that's like, there are eight things to do right now that are emergency level things to do to handle your situation. Then you move into 35 ways to attract money almost instantly. I guarantee you haven't thought of them. At least not all of them. I also talk about what are the top 10 limiting beliefs about money. You need to know those and wipe those out. I also talk about the sole purpose of money. I also talk about how a lot of people secretly sabotage their success. Also talk about how to operate your brain by using the reticular activating system and programming it to get more of what you want to have, do, or be. All of that and more is in this book. What I've tried to do is take you from stress to success, to a spiritual awakening.

Joe Vitale:

I'm all about awakening. I wrote another book called the Awakened Millionaire. It's not about the money, it's about the mission. It's about making a difference. Go to moneylovesspeedbook.com, take $2 with you and expect miracles like my signs say. And then finally, as I have one-minute left, I again want to thank Raymond. He is doing a mission of nobility by doing all of this, two days worth of information and 19, I believe some speakers here that are all contributing. Raymond, thank you for doing this. Thank you for the honor of including me in this. I am always grateful to you and for everybody watching, thanks for giving me the time. My 30 minutes of fame and fortune and Godspeed to all of you.

Raymond Aaron:

Joe, I love you more than ever. You did a great job. And you know what I teach, I teach never add time and I teach speed of implementation. And that's your first love, money is speed. I love it. I love it. I love it. And also looked up on YouTube *Look For The Light*.

Joe Vitale:

Yes. You've got *Look For The Light*, my song. Yes, it's on my album, The Great Something. Thank you for that. That's very flattering. You took a moment to do it. Thank you.

Raymond Aaron:

Thank you. You did such a beautiful job, Joe. I'm inspired by you. I love your laws. I love them. I have never thought of it that way. I really . . . It's so beautiful.

Joe Vitale:

Excellent.

Raymond Aaron:

Thank you, Joe. You're a master and you tied for a top spot amongst all the speakers sharing. So you really exhibit the giving back and the prosperity and the sharing. You're a noble human. Thank you. I'm honored to know you.

Joe Vitale:

Thank you.

How to Avoid Fear and Extra Real Dangers During This Lockdown

Justin Criner

Raymond Aaron:

. . . mine, who is a policeman in Texas. And he's going to be talking to us about what the heck's going on. What are the bad guys doing right now? Justin Criner. Can you adjust the angle, so you don't look like a midget, because you're such a big guy? There we go.

Justin Criner:

How are you, Raymond?

Raymond Aaron:

Wonderful. And just before I give you your time, I do want to announce the winners of the sharing contest. Amongst the staff, and the staff can't win because they're staff, Francis Ablola, not surprisingly, was number one. I was number two. Nancy Horse, our newest staff member, was number three and Danielle, my own executive assistant was number four. Amongst the speakers, the third place was Ruth, who's going to be on later today, and Marie Diamond and Joe Vitale tied for number one. But here's the big one.

Raymond Aaron:

Here's the top 20 shares amongst the participants, which is unbelievable because they come from nine different countries around the world. Number 20, Janet Santillan from the United States. Number 19, Nessa Ventara from Morocco. 18, Fatima Swallet from Canada. 17, Hailey Patry from Canada. 16, Sherry Gideons from the United States. We're getting close to number one. Number one wins a prize worth 10,000 US dollars. Number 15 is Rob Provenzano from Canada. Number 14, Anna Geary from England. Number 13, Ugba Chuck Wameka from Nigeria. Number 12, Dr. PPP, Privan Patel from Canada. Number 11, Anastasia, she never gave us her last name, from Slovenia. Number 10, Lukthawit Areersda from Thailand.

Raymond Aaron:

Number nine, Manal Shavani from England. Number eight, Baya Montaine from Romania. Number nine, Ruth Therbray from Canada. Number six, George Parvanov from Bulgaria. Number five, Danna Coil from America. She wasn't even on the top 20 yesterday, and she landed at number five. Number four, David Dye from Canada. Number three, Dominick Mills from England. Number two, Mira Conachevia from Bulgaria. And number one, from Canada, Mandana. Mandana, my dear friend, Mandana, number one, a prize worth 10,000 US dollars and also my heart. To the top 20 sharers, I love you. Thank you for sharing from your heart. I didn't know that I had some dear friends in Canada, Bulgaria, England, United States, Romania, Thailand, Nigeria, Slovenian, and Morocco. I didn't know that people loved me and were so intent on helping and creating this amazing event from all over the world. I'm so moved.

Raymond Aaron:

And Justin, you probably have been watching. We've had superstars in the movie, The Secret, and many of your friends, because Justin is not only a policeman. He's also an amazing entrepreneur. And I have the honor of helping him. I coach him a bit here and there. I really love him and I love helping him. I love hearing how well he's doing. And he's also a member of transformational leadership council with Jack Canfield, Dr. John Gray, and some of the other superstars that you've been watching. And so he's a noble soul, a wonderful character. And here he is, Justin Criner. So, say hello.

Justin Criner:

Hello, Raymond. Thank you for having me. This is exciting.

Raymond Aaron:

Yes. And the reason you're here is because when times are normal, we know what to do. When times are normal, we know what to do. Women don't walk late at night in bad areas of the town through an unlit park. Women know that. And we all know lock the windows, lock the doors, put on the alarm system. When you leave home for an extended time, tell your neighbors to watch over. We know that. But when times are interpolated, when times are all mixed up, holes open up and bad guys see them first. So Justin, I don't want this to be a negative talk, but I want it to alert people. What's going on from your side of the badge?

Justin Criner:

Perfect. Thank you. Great intro. So right now, many people are afraid of the extra dangers associated with civil unrest, and especially with this pandemic. This is highly evidenced to the huge spike in gun sales that we're seeing right now in the US. Do you know that gun stores in the US have been labeled as essential and gun sales have skyrocketed? Isn't that crazy?

Raymond Aaron:

Crazy.

Justin Criner:

Yeah. So people want to feel safe. Yeah, go ahead.

Raymond Aaron:

In Canada, I was shocked that liquor is deemed an essential service, but guns, no. Canadians don't do guns like Americans.

Justin Criner:

Right.

Raymond Aaron:

It's shocking that-

Justin Criner:

So people want to feel safe. And they're concerned that this world is becoming less safe and some people are thinking, maybe if I buy a gun, I'll feel safe. People are stockpiling guns. They're stockpiling ammo. They're stockpiling emergency supplies. They're even stockpiling toilet paper. I thought this was interesting. People searched for the term home safety over 40% more in March than they did in December. That's a huge increase on Google. Gun increased 35%. Help increased 33%. And survival increased 40%. What's going on? So I want to do something real quick. Everybody take a deep breath. Let out a sigh of relief.

Justin Criner:

I believe in personal protection and I believe in being safe. However, this world is a safe place. We're bombarded daily with the dangers of the world, but in reality, we're living in the safest time in history. Did you know that? It's true. We don't hear people talk about it much. So take a breath and enjoy a little peace, knowing that we really are in a safe world. That's not to say there aren't dangers out there and that's not to say there aren't new dangers, but we are not going to live in fear. We're going to live in peace. To center on this concept for a moment, I'm going to read a few quotes. Don Miguel Ruiz, who we know, "Death is not the biggest fear we have. Our biggest fear is taking the risk to be alive. The risk to be alive and express what we really are."

Justin Criner:

Dorothy Thompson said, "Only when we are no longer afraid do we begin to live." H. Jackson Brown Jr., "Don't be afraid to go out on a limb. That's where the fruit is." And James F Byrnes, "Too many people are thinking of security instead of opportunity. They seem to be more afraid of life than of death." And lastly, a phrase I like to tell myself, I can harm myself, but my injuries are not physical ones. The only way I can harm myself is through negative thoughts and negative actions and fearful thinking. However, outside of this, there's no possible way for me to harm myself because I am eternal. Remember you are not your fears. Now, doesn't it feel better to look at peace instead of fear? Doesn't it feel better to look at the opportunity instead of the risk? And isn't the shift in perspective enlightening?

Justin Criner:

And I'm not saying to abandon caution, but a peaceful, supportive perspective change is healthy, and a stressful fear state is unhealthy. As a police officer, people ask me regularly, should I be worried? It's kind of interesting, they'll call and they'll say, "Officer, should I be worried? I saw five police cars on my street," or, "I heard crime is up," or, "I heard something bad happened in my neighborhood. Should I be worried?" I always find it funny that people are asking me how much they should worry, as if I'm going to give them permission on how much they should be in fear and how much they should worry. And that's not really what they're asking. They're asking should they be concerned? Is there a major problem? But the words they're using, which are important, are saying, "Should I be worried? Should I take on negative emotions in my life?" And the answer is no, you should not be worried right now or in your daily life, but you should be prepared. And we'll talk about a little bit of preparedness and you should be vigilant. You should be happy and you should be at peace.

Justin Criner:

And this is a more natural state than worry. The world right now can seem overwhelming if you focus on that. And it's interesting to me that the things I was worried about in January don't seem to matter much today. Have any of you noticed this? A whole perspective shift has occurred in our world. Stop and think for a moment. When you feel your concerns from before the virus outbreak, are they the same as what you feel today? The world and life have the ability to trap us into a worry and fear state. It's our happy and natural place is an opportunity and a peace state, and the media wants to trap us in this fear state because that sells and that keeps us tuned in. It's like crack cocaine. We can't get rid of it.

Justin Criner:

So it's important to refocus on what's important and who's in control of your life. And I would like to talk about things that you can do to be safe, because you literally are in control of your life. Do you feel that way? Do you feel right now that you are in control? Because you are, literally you and no one else. You choose today and each minute, what you focus on, how you feel, what actions you take, what you read and what news you watch. Are you feeling that a shift needs to be made? Does your emotional gas gauge need to be filled back up? Or if you drive a Tesla, does it need to be recharged? Has the last month drained your resources? Fear is only created in your head. Fear is not external to you. It's internal. What we are fearing is probably not going to come true. And even if it does, what will happen, you will move on. You will get through it. You'll get over it. You can do this.

Justin Criner:

I love talking about overcoming fear and I could talk about removing fear all day, but I want to talk specifically about five actions to protect yourself during this pandemic. We'll talk about physical security and more importantly, we'll also talk about your mental security. First thing we'll talk about is more on the mental side and then we'll get into the physical side. Number one, the first action, take care of yourself. This is a fascinating concept to me. There are people in jail that feel free and there are people in society that feel imprisoned. Why is there a difference there? Do you feel free right now? Personal freedom is less about where you physically are and more about where you mentally are. Everyone suffers emotionally and mentally from time to time. Even the richest highest producers in the world suffer mental struggles. Even the wealthiest people in the world sometimes struggle to pay their mortgage payment. Isn't that wild?

Justin Criner:

During the 2008 financial crisis, suicide spiked. Over 10,000 people committed suicide that was directly related to the '08 crisis. A majority of people are being impacted by this in multiple ways, most of us included. We're all losing income. We're all losing close connections we have with others, losing physical freedoms. These are major life disruptions. If you're feeling down, unhappy, or not your full self, what do you need to do to get over this bump? Your mental anguish and pain is very important to heal. I want you to know that I'm here with you. If you know what you can do better, take action. If you don't know what you can do better, please ask. Ask anyone you trust, get assistance. If you are not feeling 100%, there are five simple things that will help you back to getting feeling better. And Joe Vitale touched on these, which is awesome because we didn't network any of this.

Justin Criner:

So the first one is be grateful. I believe gratitude is the ultimate reset button. Show gratitude many times a day. See the amazing creations, love, people and success around you. Enjoy these things deeply and feel in your body the power of gratitude. I have a three-year-old right now and we bless our food before every meal. And he wants to say every single prayer. And his prayers are amazing because he says, "Heavenly father, bless. Thank you for red and thank you for yellow and thank you for blue and thank you for water and thank you for air." How often are we grateful for air? How often are we grateful for the beautiful colors around us? And the three-year-old sees those things that we don't see. Sit down and get into some gratitude. It'll change your life.

Justin Criner:

Number two, avoid judging. It only brings you down. Eliminate complaints, number three. When I complain, it just perpetuates the same problems over and over. Number four, be around positive people. And number five, forgive yourself and forgive others. Now, have you ever noticed that the same people tend to be victims over and over again? This is kind of fascinating to me. It's something I've studied a little bit because you have the same people getting broken into or being in a bad relationship over and over. So why is this? We all give off vulnerable signals from time to time, and bad people take these signals as permission to attack us. People who appear in control with higher confidence and self-awareness, tend to be less likely to be victimized. So it's true that there's some people that are victimized more than others. And of course, we don't want to be victimized. This has been documented over and over again in psychological papers and publications. Psychology Today has a very long article on it if you wanted to Google search it.

Justin Criner:

To help avoid being a victim, remember the world is a safe place. Live in that mindset, but be prepared as far in advance for the unsafe. There are truly evil people in this world. Treat everyone with a contained trust. That means you don't walk around and you don't distrust everyone, but you just contain your trust and you keep it in safe boundaries. That's what we do when we put things in a safe and invite people to our house. We're trusting them into our house, but we're not trusting them into our safe. We're containing our trust.

Justin Criner:

I'm going to give you four actions guaranteed to make you feel safer and proven to help you not get victimized. These are things that they have said, "Okay, people that display these actions don't get victimized as much." The first one is walk with a purpose. When you're walking down the street, act like you're going somewhere. Second one is be vigilant in observing your surroundings. Third one is show confidence and strength as you perform daily actions. Confidence is the change between you getting attacked and not getting attacked. Don't let hype and emotion make decisions. Take your time. People that try to trick you into making a quick hype emotion decision are the ones that might take advantage of you.

Justin Criner:

So, number one thing was taking care of yourself. All that's under take care of yourself. The next step is taking care of your family. Your first support in defense to difficulties should be your family. If you're in a healthy relationship, this is one of the most important places to focus your energy. What are you doing during this time to strengthen your family relationship? Since this lockdown started, there's been an uptick in domestic violence. Many people don't have a great home life. If you know somebody that is struggling with relationship or family issues, please reach out to them regularly, more than you normally would. They need your help. If this is you, please don't continue to accept an unhappy home life as the norm, or as the standard. You can have an amazing home life. If you're struggling, get help. There are many resources out there. Living in a difficult family environment is emotionally draining and damaging, as many of us know from firsthand knowledge.

Justin Criner:

Many times people feel trapped for several reasons. I've seen people can't move because of their finances or their children, or because of threats of violence. Even if you feel like you can't get out of your home, you can still talk to somebody. There's lots of resources out there. You can still get help. You can still take small steps daily to improve your situation. If you need the strength to take the first step, ask somebody you trust to support you. I'm here as your cheerleader. I've worked with literally thousands of domestic abuse and verbal abuse and dysfunctional families. I've seen the damage it can do to children. I lived in this environment myself, as part of my childhood. You can do this. If you need help or resources, please ask for help.

Justin Criner:

Take more time during this period to spend time with the family. Do activities that are legally allowed in your area. If you can go on bike rides, talk, decompress. If you're having financial problems, compartmentalize those with the family. Don't let the money affect the family life. Money is one of the biggest problems in the family life. But I think this is interesting, if you were tomorrow, if you were living in a cardboard box, could you still be happy? Is it possible to be happy and living in a cardboard box? Can you still be with those you love? Can you see that your financial state survives independently of your happy state? So let the stress of the financial wash away. Don't let the external control the internal. Take care of your family, and your family is the biggest things you can do right now to stay safe.

Justin Criner:

The third thing, and now we're getting less into the mental and more into the physical. Online security. Lots of hackers are exploiting this. Hackers are sending out messages about government loans, jobs, test kits, et cetera, with the goal that you click on the messaging, compromising your computer or your phone. These are called phishing attacks. So you'll get an email and it'll look like it's from somebody important and it's not. And you'll click on it and you'll download a virus to your phone. The FTC and the secret service both have released tips on how to avoid these scams. Number one is don't click on links from sources you don't recognize. Number two is be mindful of emails or websites you're not familiar with claiming to have current information about the virus. There was a map that some of you may have seen that showed the virus around the world. And there were some hackers that took that map and they embedded a computer virus into the map, and people were downloading this virus when they were looking at the coronavirus.

Justin Criner:

Ignore online medical offers, such as ads touting prevention, treatment, or claims of a cure. Watch out for pressure to donate to charities in the form of wiring money or paying with gift cards. If you receive any suspicious emails, calls, texts, notify your IT department if you work for a company, or if you don't, if you just do it for yourself, delete the messages and block the sender on your personal email. And number four thing to be safe is physical security at home. How safe is your home? Have you done a security assessment of your home? If you're stuck at home, this is a good time to beef up the security. There are many things you can do to strengthen your home for low cost.

Justin Criner:

The most common place a burglar enters the home is through the front door. A lot of people believe they come through windows and they don't, very rarely. Almost 90% of burglars come through the door. How secure are your doors? Door jams on most doors are very insecure. Do you have a door jam reinforcement on your door? The number one security device your house should have before an alarm, before cameras or anything else, is door jam reinforcement. The large majority of burglaries happen when no one's home. So if you're stuck at home, you're much safer than you probably think you are. According to one study, I love this, security yard signs lower your chance of being burglarized by 80%, not having an alarm, but just having the sign put in your front yard you can get on eBay and you can buy a sign for 30 bucks and put in your front yard, an 80% reduction in the chance of you being burglarized, for $35 for the rest of your life.

Justin Criner:

Okay. Dogs in your house, cameras, alarms, and people all lower your chance of being burglarized. Burglars like places to hide. Bushes and trees where they can hide. So if you trim those away, it'll lower your chance of being burglarized. And last, do you have a family security plan? Talk to your family about security. Do you open doors to strangers? Ask these questions. Do you open doors to strangers? What do you do if someone tries to break in while you're at home? What do you do if there's a fire? What do you do if you come home to an open front door? Where and how do you store valuables? Do you have firearms in your house? And if so, how are they secured? Who knows where they are? Who is allowed to use them? Has firearm safety been taught to all members of your family?

Justin Criner:

It's concerning to me as a police officer that right now, it seems like politically we're really talking about firearms in general and how to background checks and things like that. But what happens is we don't talk about security of the firearm in the home, which is the biggest way that criminals get guns is by breaking into homes and stealing them. How are you securing your firearm? What neighbors would you go to in an emergency? Have you talked to them about making a security plan with your neighbors? Your home security is your responsibility. Please ask me if you have security questions about how to beef up your home. You can do it for very inexpensive. There's lots of things you can do.

Justin Criner:

The number five, the last thing we're going to talk about, is child online safety. I've heard rumors that children are being targeted even more right now. They're on devices more. They're not at school. They're at home. Do you talk to your kids about online safety? Do you know what your kids are looking at online and what they're being exposed to by their friends? I won't go into all the details on it because the FTC has a great website, Protecting Kids Online, and it's got links you can click on, and it talks about all different topics. It talks about cyber bullying and talking to your kids about online safety. It talks about mobile phones and kids and socializing online. It talks about virtual worlds. It talks about sexting and texting, video games, parental controls and protecting your child's privacy. So if you go to FTC website and search for protecting kids online, you'll find great links and articles on that.

Justin Criner:

So we've talked about a bunch of different things, safety things. Take a deep breath. Notice the safety and peace around you. You really are taken care of. You really are. You're really amazing. Be the light to those in need, and you will receive that light back. I'm going to go back over the five tips I have. Take care of yourself. Take care of your family. Take care of your online safety. Look at your physical security, your home. And look at your children's safety. Those are the biggest areas I see right now that are getting exploited by evil people.

Justin Criner:

The last thing I want to close with is this may be the best time in our lives for opportunity. Be safe, be open and take action for the next opportunity coming your way, because there are going to be some amazing opportunities coming around the corner from this event. You've learned some cool things the last two days. Thank you for taking action to make a wonderful world. Raymond, do you have any questions?

Raymond Aaron:

I'm speechless. It's a very, very bad reputation for a professional speaker to be speechless. For a day and a half so far, I've been listening to the top speakers in the world, and I cried during your talk. I was so moved. You speak with such authority and with such tenderness and such caring and such love. I'm so moved. Thank you so much for your presentation.

Justin Criner:

Thank you.

Raymond Aaron:

I wasn't exactly sure what it would be like. I didn't know if I'd made a mistake, if you'd have enough content or if you'd do well. I didn't know, but I had an idea that I wanted to express something within these two days along the topic that you're so familiar with. And wow, you did a brilliant job. Wow. I'm really moved. So we do have time. Francis, are there some questions that you could highlight? Francis is my genius co-collaborator, internet techie, webmaster, internet guru. Francis?

Francis:

Yes. There's a slight delay. So if anybody has questions, let us know. I'll put it in the text chat, but we'll have to catch up. There's about a minute or two delay.

Raymond Aaron:

So let me just ask you a question. Are you busier than ever or are you sequestered at home? What's going on for you?

Justin Criner:

I'm working like normal. There's been some big changes in the police world, at least where I live, and I assume worldwide. So the type of calls we're doing, the type of things we're doing, have changed. For instance, traffic enforcement is way down. Police officers just aren't stopping people. They don't want to put people at risk and it's not worth it. And I see people speeding all day long because they know they can get away with it. So I'm not giving permission, I'm just saying.

Justin Criner:

One thing that's changed where I live is our nursing homes have been so susceptible to this virus that we have officers guarding the front and back of every nursing home in town, not letting people in and not letting people out. They have to sign waivers if they want to leave, if the people in the nursing home want to leave. It's put a big toll on our resources at our police department to be able to cover that. But in the city I live in, we've had a huge outbreak in nursing homes, and other places have seen the same thing. So that's one thing we're trying to do to protect.

Justin Criner:

A couple other things people have asked me recently is about civil unrest and martial law. These seem to be hot topics. People are asking, can they really close my business down? And the answer is for the most part, yes they can. And in the US, that's more state dependent than federal dependent. And I don't know outside of the US, but I imagine they even have more powers outside the US. People are also asking, can they just pull me over for driving down the street? And in Texas, no, but I think some other states have done some different things, but in Texas, if you're going to the grocery store or going to do what you do, I can't just stop you without a reason. I need probable cause to pull you over.

Raymond Aaron:

So the big takeaway from your half hour is if you're going to speed, go for it. If you've always wanted to speed right down the main street, this might be your last chance. Francis, you've got some questions?

Francis:

Yes. One question is what were the four steps again? Walk with purpose, and then . . . Can you repeat the four steps?

Justin Criner:

Yeah, so the four things to help you, they're actually proven to make you safer, which is really fascinating to me because they did research on this. So they are . . . Let me get to that real quick. Give me a second. Sorry. Back in my notes. Okay. Walk with a purpose is the first one. Be vigilant in observing your surroundings. Look around, know what's going on around you. Show your confidence and strength as you perform daily actions. Confidence is one of the biggest things that keeps you from getting attacked. When I walk into a bad situation, like a huge fight at a bar, a huge bar fight, the difference between me and the next guy is the confidence I take in there. And I go up to the biggest guy in there and I take confidence with me and I'm able to end that situation quick, but if you walk in and you're like, "Oh, I don't know if I can handle this," you won't be able to handle it. Confidence makes all the difference in the world in you being a victim or not.

Justin Criner:

And the last thing is don't let hype and emotion make decisions for you. Don't get caught up in the emotion of what's going on right now and sell the farm or throw the baby out with the bath water, so to speak, but take a second, take a breath and get into who you are instead of letting the emotion make the decision.

Raymond Aaron:

I love what you said, that it's exactly the same people that get hit by a truck, that get hit by their husband or wife, that get burglarized. People attract the bad guys. It's strange.

Justin Criner:

It is.

Raymond Aaron:

Well, I'm glad that you're a good guy and I'm glad you're protecting us.

Justin Criner:

I'm glad to be here. Thank you very much, Raymond.

Raymond Aaron:

You did a super wonderful job. I'm so honored.

Justin Criner:

Thank you.

Breakthrough to New Levels of Success

Jack Canfield

Raymond Aaron:

Jack Canfield, if you had been living under a rock for the last 100 years, Jack is the co-creator of the Chicken Soup for the Soul series of books which has sold over half a billion copies worldwide. He's the author of The Success Principles and then 10 years later, the 10th anniversary of The Success Principles updated and revised and recently he just published this month The Success Principles Workbook at thesuccessprinciplesworkbook.com.

Raymond Aaron:

And he was the superstar of the movie The Secret, and he was the founder and creator of Transformational Leadership Council, which has now grown to be a beautiful cherished organization of a hundred of the top transformational leaders in the world. He's on the board of directors, he's indeed the chairman of the board of directors and I'm honored to be on that board with him. He has way, way more accolades than I could ever imagine.

Raymond Aaron:

He has a Guinness book of records that will never ever be broken, the New York Times list, the top 10 books of that week. And if you get on, it's a miracle. I've been on once, it was a miracle. But if you get on twice in the same week, it's unheard of. How can you be on it twice? Maybe you got a good book and it brought up the other books, so maybe you could be on twice. Jack Canfield has the record. He had seven out of the 10 books in one week on the New York Times. Seven of the 10. It's unheard of. It'll never ever be broken. Jack, take it away. Jack unmute yourself, put your video on.

Jack Canfield:

I can't put my video on, there's some thing. But the question is if we can share my screen. There's a thing that yesterday we were able to share my screen. I have a slide show that I can take people through.

Raymond Aaron:

Jack your screen is on.

Jack Canfield:

You can see my purple shirt?

Raymond Aaron:

Yeah, I can see your purple shirt.

Jack Canfield:

Okay, perfect. Then let's go. So I'm going to share with you today the success principles that I basically teach. We're going to talk about, not all of them of course, because my book has 64 success principles in it, but I want to share the basis of a system that if you apply it, you can create success in any area of your life. And as Raymond knows, I always start with cartoons. So when we laugh, we secrete endorphins that increases our immune system, which is good right now with the COVID panic going on, a pandemic going on. I guess there is a panic as well as a pandemic.

Jack Canfield:

But if you look at the screen, here we go, you see two teachers or two old ladies rather talking about their computers. One says, "My memory really sucks Mildred. So I'm changing my password to incorrect. When I log in with the wrong password my computer will tell me your password is incorrect." It says, you can name her whatever you like, but be sure it's something you can remember. You'll be using it as a security question to answer for the rest of your life.

Jack Canfield:

Wilson, an Australian sheepdog is now working from home like the rest of us are. That has to do with the pandemic as well. So the way karma works, and here we are now. We're the ones in the cage. Says, my hands have had so much alcohol on them I think they're going to have to go to rehab when this is over. I know. Isn't that funny? It says dear 2020, none of this shit was on my vision board.

Jack Canfield:

It says homeschooling is going well. Went too far too fast. Let me go back. Two students suspended for fighting and one teacher fired for drinking on the job. And a lot of us are doing this these days. Unfortunately, we know the alcohol sales are way up. Says, last month you people just are glorified babysitters when the teachers were on strike. And now it's, hey, take all the money. The kids are freaking out all over the place so are the parents. Now with social distancing, we're going to have to repaint the [inaudible 00:04:19] chapel.

Raymond Aaron:

It's great.

Jack Canfield:

And I love this. Go back again. Coronavirus baptism. Why is it not moving? No, my computer just froze. This is not okay. There we go. It says Zoom meeting, audio only, Zoom meeting with video. A lot of us have been doing that lately. So Raymond, I just have a question. Is my GoToWebinar control panel showing on the screen?

Raymond Aaron:

No.

Jack Canfield:

Just the slides. Okay, perfect. So it says life is a combination lock, your job is to find the right sequence of numbers in the right order, you can have anything you want. And so literally what I teach you guys is how to have the right numbers in the right order called success, you can unlock this combination. Now everything I'm going to teach you today comes from three sources, my book, The Success Principles, my book, The Success Principles Workbook, and also a course called Breakthrough to Success Online.

Jack Canfield:

And I'll let you know about all those later if you want to participate and go deeper in all of this. But I'll give you as much as I can in the time we have. The promise I make people when they read my books, take the courses are: you can double your income, you can double your amount of free time, you can dramatically improve any area of your life. You can create more balance in your life between work, family and self time, and you can increase your level of happiness.

Jack Canfield:

Most of my students complete that within two years, doubling their income. I've had people do it in six months. One person up in Canada now spends six months a year in Mexico in the winter and six months in the summer in the construction business where before he was working 12 months a year making half the money he makes now. And I want you to take notes as we go along, the first principle is take 100% responsibility for your life and your results. Notice it says 100%, not 99%.

Jack Canfield:

Imagine being married to someone who's 99% committed to monogamy. That would not be a good idea. So the same thing. I have a chapter in my book called 99%'s bitch, 100%'s a breeze. If you're 99% committed to running every day, every day you wake up, you have to decide whether or not you're going to run or not. I remember when Raymond was training for his polo race and he was running stairs in a hotel. And one day I think you ran for six or eight hours, Raymond, just nonstop.

Jack Canfield:

And it was never a question of only going to get up and do that today, it's called I'm doing it, I'm committed. My life's going to be on the line out there on the ice. There's polar bears and I want to make sure I don't freeze to death or get eaten. And so the reality is you have to be 100% committed. Everyone I know who has been super successful, and I've interviewed probably 250 of the most successful people in the world, mostly in North America, but around the world, billionaires, millionaires, generals in the army, people that have made bestselling books, movie producers and directors, movie stars, bestselling authors, et cetera.

Top salespeople, successful entrepreneurs, they all take 100% responsibility. They're not blamers and complainers. That is an amazing formula. And if you only write one thing down today, I would encourage you to write this down. E+R=O. This is the formula for success. If O is the outcome, events happen, response to the event that you have creates an outcome. So an event occurs, you then respond to it by what you think, the stories you tell yourself about it, the meaning you make about it, those are all thoughts, the pictures you put in your head and also what you say and do, your behavior.

Jack Canfield:

So that's the only thing you can control, your thoughts, your behavior and the images in your mind. And so basically the event is a neutral event. And we see that a lot of people will go through a recession, will go through a lockdown, will go through a sheltering at home, go through a pandemic and they come out richer, happier, maybe thinner, more successful. Other people don't. What is the difference?

And so I was asking for years, what is it that successful people are doing that's different than the other people? Putting the practice in my own life, becoming a multimillionaire, bestselling author in the process and also training hundreds of thousands if not millions of people around the world, I've given workshops in 51 different countries around the world. And the reality is that this has worked for me, it's worked for the hundreds of thousands of students that I've taught.

Jack Canfield:

So basically, everything you're currently experiencing is an outcome of how you responded to an earlier event. If you don't like the outcomes you're getting, what you have to do is change your response. And most of us are doing habits, we're not really doing new behaviors. We're stuck in the things we've been doing for 20, 30 years and what we do instead of changing our responses, we blame the event. And when you do that, you're powerless.

Jack Canfield:

The power you have is your responsibility, the ability to change your response. Now, two plus two is four, event plus response equals four. All of a sudden, the Coronavirus comes along and it's doing a one instead of two. We can't get out of our homes many of us. We find that our businesses are shut down. We might've lost our job or furloughed or much more difficult right now. We're working with kids at home or our spouses at home. We're sharing two computers among four people. There's more connection.

Jack Canfield:

John Gray talked yesterday about how we're all bumping up against each other and how that affects our relationships. Resentment and annoyance builds up. But we're getting three now. Before we were getting four, we were happy with four. But the universe, when it does two or it does one rather, we've got to change if we want to get a four. And now we've got to do something different, our response has to change and that's what this whole summit has been about.

What are some of the responses to your diet with JD Virgil? What are some of the responses to exercise, to the security that Justin just talked about, to investing strategies that we talked about yesterday, et cetera. We have to change our responses. You're getting a lot of ideas of what to do. Now the Coronavirus is an event and the outcome you're going to experience is how you respond to it. And most of you are going to have to change what you've been doing in order to get more. So we're going to talk about how to do that.

Jack Canfield:

So first of all, blaming is a response to an event. And you have to give up all blaming. Think of all the things we blame. We blame the economy, we blame the prices, we blame Wall Street. We blame the top 1%. If it wasn't for them, there'd be more money to share. We blame the president, the prime minister, the governor, the Congress, the government itself. Donald Trump blames the media. The Democrats blame the Republicans, Republicans blame the Democrats. Everyone blames people who don't vote.

Jack Canfield:

We blame the traffic for making us late. We blame the weather. We blame the Coronavirus. Our computer systems, Zoom webinar crashed yesterday. So the reality is, we tend to blame things. In America, we're blaming the immigrants. We're blaming Mexico, we're blaming India, we're blaming Iran, we blame China. For a while the Coronavirus was called the Chinese virus. We blame our competitors, we blame OPEC. Right now the Saudis and the Russians are having a fight about oil and all the prices are going down.

Jack Canfield:

But most importantly, most of us blame our boss. We blame our team members, we blame our parents, our husband or wife or children, our neighbors. All those blamings are responses. You're blaming things that are outside of you, most of which you have no control over whatsoever. And we call this victim consciousness because you think they're responsible for your experience.

Jack Canfield:

Now, Teddy Roosevelt said, if you could kick the person in the pants responsible for most of your trouble, you wouldn't sit for a month. And so literally we are responsible. You're going to have to assume responsibility. I want you to point to your temples of your head. And I know this sounds silly and weird, but it's powerful when you say it out loud. I want you to say the words on the count of three, if it's meant to be, it's up to me. Here we go. One, two, three. If it's meant to be, it's up to me. And it really is.

Jack Canfield:

If you want more money, more health, more relationship fulfillment, whatever it is, you're the one that's going to have to do it. And I mentioned that E+R=O. There're are only three Rs, your behavior, your thoughts and your images. I want to show you something very powerful about the power of your own thoughts. We'll do a quick experiment. I want you to take one of your hands. It doesn't matter which one, and I want you to look at the base of your palm.

Jack Canfield:

You'll notice there's a little line that goes across. It's kind of a wrinkle you have there. And I want you to look on your other hand, you also have the same wrinkle. And I want you to line them up and put it your hands together so that you're putting one on top of the other, kind of in that prayer position. And then roll your hands up. And if you roll your hands up, you're going to notice that one of your hands is slightly longer than the other.

Jack Canfield:

So you've taken your hands, you've put those two lines together, you've then rolled your hands up so the palms are facing each other. And I notice on my hand, my left hand rather is a little bit longer than my right hand. I want you to then take your shorter hand and put it about 12 inches in front of your face. If you're going to look at that shorter hand and we're going to say out loud in unison, eight times, grow longer on the count of three. Here we go.

Jack Canfield:

I know this is weird, but do it because it's going to show you something very powerful about the power of your intention and your thoughts. Here we go. One, two, three, grow longer, grow longer, grow longer, grow longer, grow longer, grow longer, grow longer, grow longer, very good. Now take your hands and once again line up the little wrinkles, very surgically precise like a plastic surgeon. Then roll your hands up again and notice what happened.

Jack Canfield:

And if you're like most people, you're going to find that your shorter hand actually grew a little bit longer. Now why is that? The power of our intention actually affects physical reality. And so our thoughts are controlling our physical reality much more than you realize and it controls your body, it's a major thing. When you go around saying, I'm sick or I don't feel well, you're not only describing your current reality, you're actually creating yourself feeling more sick.

Jack Canfield:

If you're focusing on the Coronavirus and thinking about how sick you'll be and what you're going to do if you do and so forth, you're actually creating your body to be more susceptible to get disease in it. Now what you can do just for drill is take that same hand, look at it, and we're just going to say in unison, back to normal six times. Here we go. One, two, three, back to normal, back to normal, back to normal, back to normal, back to normal, back to normal, back to normal.

Jack Canfield:

And if you want, you can go ahead and you can measure those hands again and see what happened. But this is just one little example. If we were in a live workshop, I'd do three or four of those things. We do muscle testing with your arm and so forth. You'd see how certain thoughts make you strong, certain thoughts make you weak. So the second principle that's critical, that's part of this combination lock of unlocking success for you is being clear why you're here, determining your life purpose.

Jack Canfield:

Well let's talk about this first. There are three ways I talk about in my books and in my trainings to clarify your life purpose. The first is a guided imagery where I literally show you how to go up a mountain, go into a temple, receive a box from a guardian angel, you're being guided in the meditative state. And you would ask for a gift that would describe and demonstrate or symbolize your life purpose.

Jack Canfield:

99% of the people who do that get something very profound. That literally for many people it's almost like changing when they realize the depth of what they're here to do. I believe every one of you is born with a purpose to fulfill, to contribute your gift to the world, your special energy, your special gift, the talents you were born with, bringing it into the world. The second thing you can do is called a cognitive approach and that's in my books. It's a six-question little questionnaire you take yourself through.

Jack Canfield:

I don't want to do that right now because it takes a little time. But in either of my books you'll find that. But something you can do today, not right this minute necessarily, but I'd like to encourage you to do it before you go to bed tonight is to take 20 minutes and sit somewhere. You can put on some very relaxing music like calm classical music or what's called environmental or ambient music, sometimes called new age music, meditation music, those kinds of things. Spa music would be another term, when you're getting a meditation.

Jack Canfield:

And just go back in time and think about when were the most joyful moments of your life. For me the most joyful moments of my life were being a teacher. I just love learning and I love teaching. And I think about seminars I've been in, ongoing courses, a month I spent on a farm in Montreal one summer learning to do psychosynthesis, which is a form of psychotherapy in workshop all day long with amazing people. 10 day for pasta meditation retreat I was in.

Jack Canfield:

I think about teaching my trainer program, all these things. I just love teaching. And so I look back and I go, "The most joy I've ever felt is being a teacher." So my purpose in life is to teach. And if I do the cognitive approach, what you see in the middle there, it comes out my purpose is to inspire and empower people to live their highest vision in a context of love and joy. So I'm inspiring you with stories like Chicken Soup for the Soul, which Raymond mentioned.

Jack Canfield:

I had seven Chicken Soup for the Soul books on the New York times on the same day. And to empower you with books like The Success Principles, courses like Breakthrough to Success and doing talks like this. And so basically that's my purpose. And when I'm doing my purpose, I experienced great joy in my life. Thomas Merton wrote, people may spend their whole lives climbing the ladder of success only to find that once they reach the top, the ladder is leaning against the wrong wall. Because often people are chasing fame and fortune rather than service.

Stephen Covey who wrote *The 7 Habits of Highly Effective People* said, if the ladder is not leaning against the right wall, every step we take gets us to the wrong place faster. And so we all know people who are millionaires and billionaires, presidents of companies, the boss of the company who are not happy, who don't have great relationships with their children, who maybe are sick a lot, who are not happy, who may be abusing alcohol and drugs or have drug problems.

Jack Canfield:

We see a lot of actors and actresses who we think have all that fame and fortune, and yet we see many of them going into rehab, their marriages ending in divorces and so forth. So success principle number three, after we've figured out and taken 100% responsibility, no longer blaming, complaining, making excuses for our life, and get clear about our purpose, what is it we want to manifest? What is our vision for our highest life expressing who we truly are? Then we want to decide what we want.

Jack Canfield:

And I'm going to share with you in a minute, something I promised yesterday that I would share with people that I learned in India about clarifying your desires, and getting really clear about what you want. But I want you to realize that once you get clear on what you want, you don't have to fully know the how to get started. Think of your inner subconscious mind as a GPS system like your car.

Jack Canfield:

I do not need to know how to drive from my house in Santa Barbara to get down to a place in van Nuys or Woodland Hills or West Hollywood. I just have to put in the address and then my car will tell me, turn right on the 101, drive for 90 miles. Get off at the West Hollywood freeway, drive for three miles, get off at this exit. I don't need to know the how, the how will show up. You'll start to learn the how. I'll describe how that happens by doing the exercise we do.

Jack Canfield:

But for this part of the seminar today, I want you to just focus on the what. Don't worry about the how. A lot of people get stuck here because they won't let themselves want what they want because they don't see how they can get it. They think they're too old. They think they're too young. They think they don't know enough people. They think they don't have enough money, enough connections, whatever it might be. But I promise you, if you're clear on the what and do what I teach you today, the how will in fact show up.

Jack Canfield:

General Wesley Clark, who used to be the commander of allied forces under NATO. He said, it doesn't take any more effort to dream a big dream than it does to dream a small dream. Think about that. You do not have to scrunch up your face harder. You don't have to burn more calories, burn more brain cells. You simply have to put another zero after your financial goal. You simply have to dream you want a bigger house, more clients, whatever it is, it's simply a choice. And once you make that choice and you do what I share with you today, you can have anything you want.

Jack Canfield:

So the question really becomes what do you really want? And while I was in India for the whole month of February with this man on the left, you'll see Dr. Naram. I was with my wife Inga, who you see on the right. That's Dr. Naram's son Krishna, who 21 years old right now, just turned 21, well, he turned 21 in May. And the guy named Clint Rogers wrote a book about Dr. Naram called the Ancient Secrets of a Master Healer, a Western skeptic in Eastern mystique and life's greatest secrets.

Jack Canfield:

And while we were there, Dr. Naram taught us about something called marma points, marma points. They're kind of like acupressure points, but they have I think even more power. They have more manifesting potential, not just medical energy movement. Anyway, what I want you to do, I'm going to teach you this real quickly, is we're going to do two different marma point exercises here that literally changed the game for me and my wife and I think it will for you too.

Jack Canfield:

One of the real problems is people often don't really acknowledge at the deepest level what they truly want. And so you can take your left thumb and finger and press on the top of your forefinger, on your right hand. But almost as if you were pressing on the point that if you're pointing and putting your pointing finger against the wall, it would be touching that point. But anywhere up in that upper point and you're going to squeeze that really hard, close your eyes and you can now squeeze that six times, one, two, three, four, five, six.

Jack Canfield:

And then keep some pressure on that point and then ask yourself, "What do I really, truly want?" And just notice what comes into your head. The first thing that comes into your mind. What do I truly, truly want more than anything? I'll be signing up for a few more seconds to see what comes. All right.

Now, whatever that is for you. For me, I just did it again today, I got the same thing I got when I was in India. I got happiness, joy, and financial independence.

Jack Canfield:

I have a lot of the things that I used to want. I've got a wonderful three-acre estate, 6000 square feet of home, and all the technology one could possibly want. I drive a beautiful Lexus, my wife drives a Mercedes. We're very, very happy in all those ways, but I noticed that the thing for me, that's the deepest thing I want is this experience of constant happiness, which I'm getting more of on as I do the inner work that I do.

Jack Canfield:

And also financial independence. I have a lot of money, but I don't have enough money to not work at all and live the lifestyle I want. Could I retire now? Yes. Could I live the lifestyle I want where I'm traveling, sending money to my grandchildren to go to private school and blah, blah, blah, blah, blah? It would take just a little more. So that's what I want. Now once you have that, what I'm going to ask you to do is, you might want to roll your sleeve up if you're wearing a shirt and put your left hand right on the base of the palm of your right arm, just like you'll see there.

And then what you're going to do is you're going to roll your hand over so you end up like that. So your hand is like you see in the first picture, you roll it over so it looks like that. And then you'll notice that you have your third finger. If you count up from your pinky finger, one, two, three, under that finger we're going to press on the arm. And this spot is a manifestation spot. And so what we're going to do is press there six times, one, two, three, four, five, six. While you at the same time, and we'll do it again, you're going to imagine that out above your right eye there is a white frame.

Jack Canfield:

And so in a moment we'll be closing our eye. We'll be imagining there's a picture frame. This image doesn't quite do it because I couldn't find the clip art I needed yet. But imagine that frame is above his right eye. So you're going to close your eyes and imagine about above your right eye there's a big white picture frame. And as you press on that spot on your arm six times, you're going to imagine a picture of what you would see as you look out your own eyes. What would you be seeing that would let you know you've achieved that goal?

Jack Canfield:

So I might be seeing a bank balance or a statement from my financial planner of what my current net worth would be. It would allow me to have the total financial freedom and never have to work again if I didn't want to and still live the lifestyle I wanted. So what would you be seeing? What would be the visual image you'd know where I made it, it's accomplished? And what would you be feeling? What would you be feeling?

Jack Canfield:

Keep visualizing that and feeling that. If you want, you can keep pressing that point. Very good. Now I want you to take your right arm. I don't have the slide for this. But take your right hand and on your left shoulder, in the front, like you're patting the front, not on the top of the shoulder, but in the front. I want you to flap your shoulder six times as you say, good job. One, two, three, four, five, six. You can also add things like, congratulations. I believe in you. I trust you. I know you can do it. If you have an affirmation, I'm so happy and grateful that we're now earning $6 million a year. Whatever it might be.

Jack Canfield:

This is very powerful, very simple technique. You can do this every day to visualize your goal once you know what that top goal is. So I share with you some really powerful ancient secrets not shared with most people out there. All right. So success principle number four, after you've got clear about what you want, it says to use your power to set a goal. So we've done that. But I want you now to take the goal you've set and I want you to set a different kind of goal. We're going to call it a breakthrough goal that would take you and quantum leap you toward the fulfillment of what you just said.

Jack Canfield:

I can't even talk. I was clearing my throat. My ultimate goal financially was to have $30 million in net worth, which would produce at 6% invested $1.8 million a year, the taxes on that would be about 6 million, I would have $1.2 million to live my life. I'm about two thirds of the way there right now. So a breakthrough goal for me would be to make personally this year, let's say $4 million. And so that would be a breakthrough goal. That would be twice as much as I made last year in terms of the net income that I made from my work.

Jack Canfield:

And so now, because I had a big sale when we sold Chicken Soup for the Soul, and my net worth went up to about 20 but now I want it to get to 30. So if I can add two a year for a couple of years, that would be a breakthrough. Or I could 10X that and say I want to make $10 million in one year, which is possible. So I want you to set a breakthrough goal that would quantum leap you toward the achievement of what you said you just really wanted.

Jack Canfield:

And I give you some examples of breakthrough goals that people in my seminars have sent in the past. Create my own five-minute radio show, write and publish a book, open up China as a market for their multilevel marketing company. Learn Spanish, Chinese, Arabic or French, depending on where you live and where you want to do business. Get an MBA degree or your realtor's license or some other certification. Double my sales, triple my income, or 10X my income. Maybe get a big client like Apple, Google, Facebook, or Uber.

Jack Canfield:

So what I'd like you to do is realize a goal has to be how much by when. So I'd like to increase my income, or I'd like to be financially independent. That's an intention, but it's not a goal or an objective. I will earn an income of $300000 by 5:00 PM April 2nd, 2021. That would be a specific measurable goal. So the key here is how much by when. You've got to be very specific, how much do you want? If it's a big house, how many square feet? Where's it located? By when? What date?

Jack Canfield:

So take a moment and just write down your breakthrough goal. I'll give you 30 seconds. It may take longer than that, but you can complete writing it while I begin talking again. So writing down your breakthrough goal. We know that when you write your goal down, it actually increases your odds of achieving it. I'll talk about that in just a minute. So I'll be quiet for 15 seconds. Write down your breakthrough goal. I will what by when?

Jack Canfield:

We know that people who write down their goal are nine times as much over their lifetime as people who don't. That was a study done by Professor David Kohl at Virginia Tech. Just the mere act of writing it down increases your odds of earning nine times more money than most people do in their life. Dr. Gail Matthews at Dominican University in Santa Rosa, California did another study where she divided people into five groups.

Jack Canfield:

Group one was simply to have a goal, not write it down, just think about it. 43% achieved their goal. Group two and three were to think about their goals, but also write down their goals. They achieved 56% of their goals. Group four was to share their goal with a friend, declare their goal to the public in some way, and 64% achieve it. But group five did all of that, but had a weekly progress report to a friend.

Jack Canfield:

They were accountable to a coach, a mentor or a friend, someone that held them accountable to actually taking the steps to achieve the goal. Notice that's a 33% increase simply by writing it down, telling someone what you could do today and then finding an accountability partner, someone you tell on a weekly basis how you're going, how you're achieving and what action steps you're taking to achieve that goal.

Jack Canfield:

What we do in our company, we practice something called the rule of five. Everyone has to write down their five top priority actions for the day and then achieve those no matter what. Sometimes people and their work day at 3:00 because they've done everything they were supposed to do. Sometimes people work till 10:00 at night because they know they got to get these five things done in order to achieve the goals. So we call this the rule of five.

Jack Canfield:

You want to do five things a day toward the achievement of your breakthrough goal. And again, having an accountability partner because most of the things you're going to need to do are going to be a little uncomfortable. Now another success principle, number six is believe it's possible, that you can do it. I love this picture of the kitten who sees himself as a tiger. And you want to see yourself doing that which you want to do. You can see it in that white picture frame we talked about above your right eye earlier.

Jack Canfield:

Napoleon Hill said, whatever the mind can conceive, that's to bake up, to think up, and believe. Belief is just a choice. You just choose to believe it's possible. You don't let external circumstances or the past tell you what's possible. You decide that it's possible for you. It's just a choice you make. You act as if you believe it and then the mind can achieve it. Cliff Young was 61 years old. He decided he wanted to run a race. There were no 10Ks, there were no marathon scheduled when he had time to do it. He was a farmer. He was a sheep farmer.

Jack Canfield:

You see him there running on his farm, in his big rubber boots. And he showed up to the race, which actually was a 544-mile race, 875 kilometers. And he'd never run a race before. And he said, "Well, the reason I signed up for this one, it's on my schedule. I could do it." They were afraid he's going to have a heart attack, but he said, "No, I'm a sheep farmer. I chase my sheep around all the time. Me and my sheep dog, we run up the sheep when there's a storm coming in. I'm a vegetarian, I eat well, sleep well, I think I can do it."

They finally let him do it. He takes off and everyone else is like young people in Nike, Reebok, Asics running gear. He's wearing that cap you see up in the top of the middle picture, he's got his boots on. And he ran that way, but he had a secret nobody knew. He didn't have the belief that you had to sleep every day. It's a six-and-a-half-day race and everyone's supposed to sleep six hours a night.

Jack Canfield:

And he didn't know that and he was so far behind the first day because he was doing this kind of shuffle that he does as opposed to really running hard out. And no one told him to go to bed. No one told him to get some sleep. And so he did that for a couple of days, no sleep and then he passed everyone one night because they were all sleeping. Again, no one told him to sleep. Anyway, he ran straight for six days without sleep and broke the record by 12 hours.

Jack Canfield:

And the next year they had I think 12 of the people did the Cliff Young shuffle, a different kind of pace and didn't sleep. And cliff came in 12th because of his age. But they renamed the race the Cliff Young Australia six-day race because it used to be the six-and-a-half-day race. So again, it's your beliefs that control you. It's not what you don't know that's so important. It's what you think you know that's not true and you have to replace those limiting beliefs with positive beliefs.

Jack Canfield:

One of the ways to do that and one of the tools for accelerating your success is under success principle number five, which is use the affirmations and visualizations. So there's a short form affirmation called I am so happy and grateful that I'm now, and then you fill in the blank. Anything you say after the words I am basically tells your subconscious, let's make this happen. And it's the most powerful two words you can say in the English language.

Jack Canfield:

So be very careful what you say after I am. I am sick, I am ugly, I am fat, I am old, all those things, and I'm going to say cancel, cancel so my subconscious doesn't hear them. All those things actually log in to you. And so you want to use it for positive. I am so happy and grateful that I'm now running a personal income of $300000 a year. One for the Coronavirus. I am so happy and grateful that I'm now experiencing vibrant health, profound happiness and inner peace.

Jack Canfield:

These are the kinds of things you want to be affirming in your life right now. And if you want to have perfect health, you want to be affirming having perfect health and peace. Mark Victor Hansen and I, when we decided we wanted to sell 1 billion Chicken Soup for the Soul books, we had an affirmation. We are so happy and grateful that we're now celebrating having sold more than 1 billion Chicken Soup for the Soul books.

Jack Canfield:

We actually got mocked up a Time Magazine cover with the two of us on it and it said Chicken Soup sells over 1 billion copies.

We post that around our office. That was on our screensavers, on our phones, on our computers. And we have now sold over 600 million books. We've had over a billion people have read the books. In China alone they've sold over 315 million books and they're using them as textbooks in the schools to teach English to the Chinese with English on one page and Chinese on the other. So we're well on our way to having achieved that goal.

Jack Canfield:

I had an affirmation for a while. I'm so happy and grateful that I'm now working with people in positions of power to create a better world. I said that affirmation for about a year and then I got invited to the White House to have lunch at the White House and afterwards I got to go down where the president does his press conferences and pretend I was the president pointing to a CNN reporter for a question and get my picture taken. So these things actually work.

Jack Canfield:

One of my affirmations I use was I'm happily to positing my million dollar royalty check from my bestselling book. And then I changed it to, I'm happily depositing my million dollar royalty check from Health Communications Inc, which became the publisher of the first Chicken Soup book. And here you'll see a royalty payment written to me for $1130328.35 cents. And that was the first million dollar check our publisher had ever written anybody. He put a smiley face in his signature because for every dollar I made he made three. So he was doing very, very well at that time.

Jack Canfield:

And that year, that was for one quarters royalty. Both Mark Victor Hansen and I, the coauthor, made $6 million just off Chicken Soup for the Soul royalties. So affirmations work if you work your affirmations. So take a moment and write down your affirmation for your breakthrough goal. I am so happy and grateful that I now am what. I'll give you about 15 more seconds to do that. All right. So we want to combine affirmation with visualization. I know a lot of people know this, this is not news to people.

Jack Canfield:

What I find unfortunately is most people don't actually do it. And so you want to have a practice of twice a day saying your affirmations. You might have two or three or four or five, however many big goals you want to focus on and then to visualize. And you can now use this technique of visualizing in that white screen that we talked about. Somehow when we look up to our right and we visualize up there, it actually has a more powerful impact on our subconscious mind and on our prefrontal cortex, which comes up with solutions, creativity, and rational thoughts that'll help us get there.

Jack Canfield:

So the daily practices. Read your affirmation, close your eyes and visualize it as complete and then feel the feelings you would feel if you'd already achieved it. You remember I asked you what would you be feeling if you've already achieved the goal. And just like an actor, put a smile on your face or have a sense of relief or calm or enthusiasm or invigoration, whatever it might be that would be the feeling you would have if you'd already achieved that goal.

Jack Canfield:

The reason this works is whenever you have a vision that doesn't match your reality and you keep visualizing it, like you're visualizing you're in Hawaii but actually you're in Toronto, what happens is it creates such structural tension in your brain. Your brain wants to resolve that tension. One reason we set a goal is the brain wants to resolve that and achieve that goal so it can relax. So the more we give it something to work on, the more it has to work to resolve the tension.

Jack Canfield:

And that creates a shift in your perception, it expands your creativity. Well, let's go back to the shift in perception for just a second. Right now, you're not aware of what you're feeling in your right foot, but as soon as I say right foot, you can feel it. So that was streaming up your leg into your spine, up your spine, up into your brain, but it was being filtered out. And your brain is filtering out lots of things, both ideas from your subconscious as well as resources in the outside environment that help you achieve your goal that you're not seeing that you would see if you're, if the brain filter was opened up and the thing that opens it up is having this structural tension.

Jack Canfield:

You get expanded creative ideas. You'll wake up in the middle of the night, you'll be in the shower, you'll be driving to work, you'll have these ideas. You'll get increased motivation to take action, and then you'll take action which produces the results. So to give you a sense of this, let's do one little shift in perception exercise just to notice something about what you see and what you don't see.

Jack Canfield:

So I want you to read this sentence out loud with me on the count of three one, two, three. Finished files are the result of years of scientific study combined with the experience of many years. Now I'm going to put that back up there and I'm going to leave it up for 10 seconds, exactly 10 seconds. I want you to count how many times does the letter F like in Frank, how many times does the letter F appear in that sense? Here we go. All right. How many Fs did you count? Did you count three Fs, four Fs, maybe five Fs, six Fs.

Jack Canfield:

Most people that I've done this with if we were in a live seminar, I put this up on a screen, they see three Fs. There are in fact three Fs that you see there, but there are six Fs. Most people don't see the Fs that are in the word of. Perhaps because we say it the of like ovens opposed to F. But if these are important things, there's all kinds of things that are outside our perceptual field that are resources and solutions to problems that many of you are not seeing.

Jack Canfield:

I call most middle class people, three F people, people like bill Gates and Steven Spielberg and Michael Dell, the lady who started Spanx is now a billionaire, Sarah Blakely. All these people see more Fs than you and I do. And so I'm seeing a lot more Fs than I used to so I'm much more successful. But there are people out there seeing even more Fs, more opportunities, more potential ideas, more potential investment opportunities, et cetera.

Jack Canfield:

So your daily routine now, your daily discipline is visualize your goals as already complete for a few minutes, twice a day and feel the feelings you would feel. One person I know that was taught this methodology had a gym. The COVID-19 shutdown came, Coronavirus, no one's allowed to go to gyms anymore. His business was tanking. He started visualizing his goal to make more money even during the pandemic.

Jack Canfield:

And then this idea occurred to him. People still want to exercise. I have the phone numbers of all my clients because when they enrolled, they filled out applications. He called them up and said, "Would you like to rent the equipment or just keep your membership going?" And so within one hour all the equipment got cleared out of his place. He delivered it, he sanitized it all. And the people were very happy to have the equipment. And then he started buying more equipment for more people who wanted it, renting it. And so he has a thriving business now where before he would have just had shuttered doors.

Jack Canfield:

So I teach something called the hour of power, which is 20 minutes of meditation every morning. Also, if you're doing your visualizations, your affirmations and the gratitude exercise just being grateful like Justin Criner talked about in the last hour. You want to make sure you fit that into that first 20 minutes. These will keep your vibration high and will give you ideas and insights.

Jack Canfield:

I love this cartoon. It says a stack of books on his bedside table he's been intending to read for years fell over and crushed him. So 20 minutes of reading every day, I want you to read for 20 minutes. Something uplifting, something that will inspire you or something that will give you . . . Like a self-help book, a motivation book, a book on psychology, a book on investing, those kinds of things. And then 20 minutes of exercise. If you do that, you're going to be healthier, wealthier, and wiser at the end of the year.

Jack Canfield:

It says I named my dog five miles so I can tell people I walk five miles every day. We're not talking about that kind of short exercise. We're really talking about getting the exercise in that you need to get in. So what's one of the main things that most separates winners from losers in life? It's called winners take action. So success principle seven is you've got to take action. You have to do the thing that you get inspired to do.

Jack Canfield:

There's two kinds of actions, obvious actions. You want to be a doctor, got to go to medical school. But there's inspired actions. Sometimes you'll be thinking, I think I'll go to that Tim Hortons or I go to that Starbucks instead of the one I normally go to. You don't know why you feel inspired to do that, or you have this intuitive hit to do it, but you do. And as you're standing in line, you meet a future client, or you meet someone that can do business with you, or perhaps you meet the next person to get married to, whatever it is. But the point being that you want to trust your intuition and take action.

Jack Canfield:

This cartoon says, step one, apply miracle cellulite cream to problem areas. Step two, run 10 miles. You've got to do the action. Remember we talked about the rule of five. Do five things every day that will lead to the achievement of your goal. Well, for me, those five things were push out Chicken Soup for the Soul, call five newspapers. See if they'll review the book in their book section or their family life section.

Jack Canfield:

Or call five radio stations and see if they would interview us on one of their talk radio shows. Or send five books to bookstores and see if they'll carry the book or send five books to the PXes on the military bases and see if they'll carry the book. But five things every single day to promote that book. We did that for 14 months before we hit a bestseller list. But as you heard in my introduction, once we hit the New York Times list, we climbed up to number one and then we stayed there for three years.

Jack Canfield:

Then Chicken Soup for the Soul 2nd Helping came out. Then a third serving, a fourth course, a fifth bowl and so forth. And we got seven books on New York Times list all on the same Sunday one day. Now I want you to do something very quickly for me. I want to show you about action. Just fold your hands like you see on the screen there. And notice which thumb is on top, your left thumb or your right thumb.

Jack Canfield:

And then what I want you to do is I want you to move all your fingers. Don't just move your thumbs, but move all your fingers. Unclasp from the above, remove all your fingers up a notch. So the other thumb automatically and naturally comes out on top. And notice how that feels. Most people say it feels awkward, feels wrong, feels yucky, I don't want to do it. I don't like it. I want to go back. So let it go back to the old way you did, the first way. Relief.

Jack Canfield:

Well, this is called a habit, the way you folded your hands the first time. And when you fold your hands a new way. Do it again, the new way I just asked you to do it with the other thumb on top. That's uncomfortable. Everything you need to do that's going to make you more successful is going to feel uncomfortable at first. And you have to get comfortable feeling uncomfortable if you want to be successful.

One of the actions you have to take is you have to ask for what you want. Ask, ask, ask, ask, ask, ask, ask. With Chicken Soup for the Soul, we had to ask 144 publishers that told us no, no, no. We had to say next, next, next, next. It was 155th publisher that said yes. 144 rejections. If I'd given up after 100, there'd be no Chicken Soup for the Soul. Raymond and I never would have written Chicken Soup for the Canadian Soul. I probably wouldn't be on this call right now. None of you would have heard of me, none of you would have cared.

Jack Canfield:

And so you never want to give up. You want to keep on asking, asking, asking until you get a yes. One of the things we did after so many no's is we said, "What would it take to get a yes?" And one publisher told us, "We need to know we can sell 20000 copies." So for a year we put out these sheets on every chair of every talk we ever gave. Sometimes 500 people, sometimes 100 people, sometimes 50, sometimes 100 and it said, I promise to buy blank number of copies of Chicken Soup for the Soul.

Jack Canfield:

And Raymond Aaron actually wrote 1000 in there. And when the book came out, we sent him that and said, "You made a commitment." And he said, "I know." And he bought a thousand books. We sold 20000 books in two weeks because we had captured all this. So we had to do a two level ask. First, ask people to promise to buy. The second we asked the publisher to trust us that we would sell those books. And as a result of that, we went on to become bestsellers.

Jack Canfield:

If Howard Schultz had given up after being turned down by banks and investors 217 times, there would be no Starbucks. 217 times people said no before he got an investor to open his first thing. So think about this, some will, some won't. So what? Someone's waiting. So you got to keep ask, ask, ask, ask, asking. And I would just end with this. Let me jump ahead to a slide here and then we'll open up the questions.

Jack Canfield:

You have to persist. Most people give up way too soon. Think about this. Michael Jordan was cut from his high school basketball team, but what did he do? He practiced all summer. He came back and he made the team and went on. He's one of the richest men. He's on the Forbes billionaire list. Michael Jordan became a billionaire playing basketball and then doing all the nourishments he does.

Oprah Winfrey was fired from her first TV job because they said she didn't know how to interview people. Think about that. That's ridiculous. Martin Luther King said, take the first step in faith. You don't have to see the whole staircase, just take the first step. So basically you have to learn more to earn more. We'll talk about that in just a moment. I want to open it up to questions for just a second or two and then Raymond and I have an offer we're going to make to you. Are there any questions that anyone has?

Raymond Aaron:

Yes. Francis, can you look for questions?

Francis:

Yes, absolutely. I'm posting that in the chat box now. First there's a couple minute delay. So as they come in, I'll let you know.

Raymond Aaron:

So while we're waiting for the delay to end, Jack, what I love is what you said in the movie The Secret, if you want to drive from California to New York, you don't have to know the whole route, you just have to see as far as your headlights go.

Jack Canfield:

That's right. Most people think they need to see the whole way, they have to have the whole thing figured out. And the trick is you just have to start. And because we have a GPS system that tells us our next step. I mean, I did not start out my career to be a world famous author. I mean, I got a C in freshmen composition in college. No one would have predicted that I was going to become a bestselling author. Now they ask me to come back and be a visiting author and talk to freshmen to inspire them about writing.

Jack Canfield:

But the point being that I couldn't see that, but if I just did the next step, became a teacher and then I became interested in self esteem and I wrote about that and then that became a bestselling book. And then people started asking me to teach adults and that became working with adults rather than just working with kids and then training adults that weren't in education and then writing the first Chicken Soup book. And then people said, "You should write another one." I just kept following my nose and doing the next thing that was in front of me. And here I am living what most people would call a pretty charmed life.

Raymond Aaron:

Yes. And this event, this World Prosper Summit, started nine days ago, nine. We got the idea. I invited my dear friends like you. We publicized it like crazy, it went viral. We broke GoToWebinar, they can't handle the numbers we're giving them. And I couldn't see any of it. I just started. So Francis, do you have questions?

Francis:

Yes. Tricks to follow through the five list. Following through on the five list.

Jack Canfield:

Repeat the question. I didn't quite understand it yet.

Francis:

So Craig is asking, what are the tricks to follow through on your five list?

Jack Canfield:

The rule of five. The trick is having an accountability partner. So you write down the five things that if you would achieve, they would take you toward your goal. And then what you do is you post that where you're going to see it. You tell someone that you're going to do it and that's why I recommend an accountability partner. If Raymond and I were accountability partners, we would call each other every morning.

Jack Canfield:

I would tell Raymond the five things I plan to do today. He would tell me the five things he's going to do to achieve his breakthrough goal. Then tomorrow I would call him and report in, these are the five things I did them or I didn't do them. No lying, no excuses, no telling him why I didn't do it. It's just called I didn't do it. Then Raymond would say, "Are you willing to recommit to that today?" And I would say yes.

Jack Canfield:

The reason that works so powerfully is that it gets embarrassing after a few days to tell people you didn't do it. And so most people listening to things like this are what we call solo entrepreneurs. You either run your own company without a boss or you're like an accountant, a coach, a lawyer, somebody that doesn't necessarily have a huge staff. You don't have a boss. And so nobody's holding you accountable to do the hard, difficult things. So we do the easy things that don't necessarily be the things that are going to get us toward the goal.

Francis:

Wonderful. We have another question here. How do you keep moving forward with this mind stuff when you tried so many times and not succeeded?

Jack Canfield:

Basically what's stopping you is what's called unconscious limiting beliefs, unconscious limiting beliefs. And if you just go to jackcanfield.com and just register to be on our list, I'm going to be doing free phone calls, three of them in the next month or two where I take people . . . I did this in January with 1000 people on each call where I led them through about a 30-minute process to identify the limiting belief that's stopping you from doing the thing you need to do to achieve your goal.

Jack Canfield:

It's a powerful, powerful tool that was developed by a woman named Lise Janelle and a friend of Raymond's. Raymond knows her very well. She's a Canadian, lives in Montreal. And also I'm adding to this now, doing it with essential oils. I'm going to do one call without, one call with. And we're finding now by rubbing essential oils on your hand and breathing certain oils while you do this, you can actually dissolve the negative affect or emotion related to a triggering event from the past.

Jack Canfield:

Maybe you cried and got made fun of or you didn't finish something and you were told you're not a finisher or you were told that when you succeed it make you bad or feel bad because he never makes metal so you don't want to make anyone feel bad. So subconsciously you never do because you never win.

So that's as much as I can tell you about it right now. But 99% of the time, it's an unconscious limiting belief that was formed between the ages of three and eight and there are powerful tools for releasing that, which I can share with you.

Raymond Aaron:

But what's most important is that Jack is going to offer you something right now that will help you eliminate your unconscious negative beliefs. Jack, please talk about this. That's amazing.

Jack Canfield:

Yes. In fact that the exercise I just talked about is in this program and it's called Breakthrough to Success Online. It's the ultimate master class that I've created for creating what you want. We keep hearing about masterclasses. I love this phrase. Success takes a while, but you can go faster with a master. If you study with someone who knows what they're doing, who's been down that road, you wouldn't want to go to Africa without a guide.

Jack Canfield:

The guide knows where the lions are, knows where the hippopotamuses are and knows where the rhinoceroses are, knows that if you keep your arms inside the Jeep, the lion's not going to eat your arm off. All these things are valuable because they've been there before and they've done what you want to do. So I have this class that's online. There's 19 hours of powerful information that you can access for the rest of your life as long as there's an internet out there in the world.

Jack Canfield:

You have lifetime access to this. You can watch it. Your family members can watch it with you. I recommend watching it with your spouse or with a child so you both can hold each other accountable and learn this, it becomes part of the culture in the family. And literally it's going to teach you to do all the things we talked about here. Tapping into your true power, discovering your true purpose, aligning with your purpose and passions, defining your dreams, probing your mind for success, activating law of attraction, taking bold and inspired action, developing new habits, which is critical.

Jack Canfield:

Creating a support community. You'll be in a Facebook group. We have a private Facebook group for everyone who joins the Breakthrough to Success Online program. You're going to have PDF action guides, all the worksheets you'll need to fill out as you go along, are downloadable. You're going to get some bonuses, 12 previously recorded Q&A coaching calls that we've done with people in this class, plus the best Ask Jack.

Jack Canfield:

For five years I did Ask Jack, you heard a couple of questions that came in there at the end and I've been doing that for years and we recorded a number of those. Plus we have tapping. If you don't know about tapping, tapping is the most powerful way to release negative emotion. Also, it's a way to help eliminate limiting beliefs. Another way you can do it besides the deep dive process I mentioned about that Lise Janelle developed that I do with her.

Jack Canfield:

So that's going to be available, a three-hour video class on tapping into ultimate success. And you also get a Breakthrough to Success Online printed workbook comes with that. So normally this would cost you 1295. And if you just go to aaron.com\success, A-A-R-O-N, that's Raymond, .com, aaron.com\success. You're going to come up to a page that looks like this and you can just fill that out and you'll see all the bonuses you're getting there, all the things that are part of it.

Jack Canfield:

And you're saving about $600. This is 695 Canadian. So if you're coming in from the US in terms of US dollars. And I will promise you that if you want to double your income, if you want to have more health, more wealth, more happiness, live the life of your dreams, this will do it. This will take you where you want to go. Raymond, do you want to add anything to that?

Raymond Aaron:

I absolutely do. Jack is a genius as a teacher. He's really clever and his most powerful in hotel workshop has been Breakthrough to Success. And he's now taken it online and instead of thousands of dollars as it normally is in a hotel, it's only 695 Canadian to get Jack for 19 hours of his vast wisdom online from the comfort of your home. It's the best deal you'll ever get. We're dear friends, he's doing it as a favor for me. Grab it, totally grab it.

Raymond Aaron:

He is a true leader, a great, great teacher, and he has the wisdom you need to move you through your unconscious inabilities, with your negative ways of thinking, even though you think, "No, I'm positive, I'm positive." Well, if you don't have all the money you want or all the help that you want or all the relationship you want, there's some parts of you that are sabotaging it. And in Breakthrough to Success Online, that will just explode away. It's the best deal you could imagine. Jack Canfield online, straight for 19 hours, you can't get anything better than that.

Jack Canfield:

And I would just add, Raymond, you have lifetime access to this. You can go back and review things. You can go back and do the processes. There are guided visualizations, there are guided meditations in this class. It's really, really profound. I promise you, this will be one of the best investments you ever made in your life.

Raymond Aaron:

And I will also promise it because Jack is one of my dearest friends and when he promises to deliver, he delivers. Aaron. com\success, Aaron.com\success. Jack, you did a dazzling job. I love you. I'm glad there was no technical difficulties today.

Me too, me too. Thank you very much. This was fun. I appreciate the opportunity to speak to your friends and all of our friends.

Being Creative Especially in Times of Great Change

Karyn Mullen

Raymond Aaron:

She is one of the top professional CEOs in the world. She can be parachuted into any company, whether it's limping along or whether it's falling or whether it's in debt, negative, losing money. And she turns it around. She has a genius ability to turn it around. She knows exactly what to do. She walks in, she looks around and she just knows. And she can increase a company's revenue by 15 to 30% a year, no matter how badly it's been limping along in the past. Companies grab her, boards of directors grab her and say, "Please work for me. Please work for me." And she turns them around. She is amazing at that. And her topic is exactly what we need during these crazy times. We need creativity. So Karyn, say hello. Karyn, I muted you?

Karyn Mullen:

Hello. There. Can you hear me now?

Raymond Aaron:

I can hear you perfectly.

Karyn Mullen:

Hi, hubby.

Raymond Aaron:

No, no. We have to be very formal.

Karyn Mullen:

Okay.

Raymond Aaron:

I'm the moderator and you are a speaker.

Karyn Mullen:

I am. Am I also on video by the way?

Raymond Aaron:

No.

Karyn Mullen:

Okay. Okay. So I will introduce myself the way that I would, which is in maybe a more modest way, is yes, people do ask me to run their business or grow their company. My however is I'm very selective in how I create my life. So I don't say yes to every opportunity. I look for opportunities and then make a place for myself. So I'm going to show you how I do it. Not because I want you to hire me. You probably can't hire me. I work for a certain . . . I'm pretty full right now. Put it that way.

But I will give you ideas and hopefully just shake you from where you are right now, so that you can have more of what you want. So we're going to talk about creativity and we're going to look at creating, combining and connecting. So I grow companies by double-digits. I'm a builder, so I understand organizations.

But I also have my own magazine and you can look at it @ firstladyglobalmagazine on Instagram, but I'll tell you more about that.

Karyn Mullen:

Okay, create. Let's just look at the basics here. So bring into existence, to cause something to happen as a result of one's actions. So it's not just imagination. It includes action. That's creativity or create. An example, nobody wants squirrels' clothes. So one of the most requested traits of a CEO is that they're creative, but it isn't this kind of creative. Creativity has to be linked to producing something of value. The same when you hire a marketing company, many times you have creative people disconnected from results. So you get pretty pictures, but not things that produce income for the organization or profit. So to be worthy, it has to go from where you are to where you want to be personally and professionally. So, that's the importance of creativity. It's finding a path, usually an alternate path to your goal. It's moving slower than I want it to. Here we go.

Karyn Mullen:

Okay, so a creative person, sometimes is seen as flaky. And one of the reasons why is because they can envision things that other people can't see. It doesn't mean it's not there, but they see it in advance. So in this example, this guy can see the ocean, but the other one can't see it. So for a creative person to basically communicate and have other people follow, you have to pair yourself with somebody, usually a PI follow through to make it real. And you need to be able to make something concrete so that people won't just think your airy-fairy.

Karyn Mullen:

One of the ways to create is to know who's creating, I call this like, let's call it your spirit or your big self. Most people get stuck and they can't create because they get stuck in one of their roles. So you have to know that you created that role. The big you created you as a wife or a husband, as a mother, as a daughter, as a doctor, but you aren't the thing that you created. And if you think that you are, you get stuck there and can't change when the environment requires you to change like now. So you're a mother, you're a lover, you're a police officer and the problem comes is if you try and be a police officer all the time, you won't create the expected result. And in this case, you can't be a great wife if you go home and you treat your husband like he's a criminal.

Karyn Mullen:

So create, it means formed out of nothing. When you create, you don't have a past. So the ability to create isn't what we see most often. Most times it is not something formed out of nothing. And even in terms of coping with the situation that we have right now, you probably won't invent the next Google. However, it doesn't mean that you can't really thrive. And I want to just get you loosened up. So experience is a terrible source of creativity. So if you look at your whole life and you look back on it and what worked, you can't actually use that as a source of creating. And the reason is you've got a lot of life ahead of you, that's where your future is. Sorry about this, you guys. I don't know why that happened. Okay, here we go. We're back.

Karyn Mullen:

So a bear . . . I'm so glad I didn't have something crazy on my screen. If a bear goes to the same part of the lake and hunts for salmon every year, and there's no salmon there, well, he's going to starve. Now, if we look at ourselves in this case, if you're just waiting for the salmon to return, in other words, waiting to go back to work and everything to be normal, it's unlikely to be true. So you have to get yourself ready that things have changed and tell yourself that you need to find new hunting territory.

So what everybody's doing right now is not what you should do. So for example, everybody is selling medical masks. That's great for now. It's, let's say hustling, but it's not going to be a long term solution. And whatever you hear everybody doing is the opposite that you should do. So you either have to invent a new fishing technique or you need to fish in a different hole than everybody else's.

Karyn Mullen:

Now here's one of the things that's a prerequisite. You cannot create a masterpiece if you're frightened. Imagine yourself in a room where you're trying to create something amazing and you know that there's a fire raging outside. Well, in this case, it's either economic ruin or you're worried about your health. And even though that might be true, you have to look at what you can do, not the stuff that could possibly go wrong, because you cannot create the future by looking at those things that you think might consume you. So fear kills your creativity and helping other people awakens your creativity. So your real solution is just to decide that you can help. And I'm just going to keep going at this.

Karyn Mullen:

So one of the ways that you can create, and you do not have to be a genius is to combine things. So you unite and merge things. And one of it is you can merge products, you can merge ideas, you can merge groups of people or companies so they act together. I'm going to give you some examples. So let's take Tex-Mex, that's Texan and Mexican, usually in terms of food. So they take the ingredients common in the South of Texas on the border and foods that are also popular in Mexico. So you take the same ingredients, but you mix them together in a different way. And what do you get? You get nachos, you get burritos. These are different foods that didn't exist in either country until the combination. Your most likely to have a breakthrough by creating your own Tex-Mex situation. So you look at two things that already exist, but haven't been combined yet. So look at your industry, look at this webinar and see what pieces of things you can mix together.

Karyn Mullen:

So what do you get when you get a lawyer plus a performer? You get Judge Judy. She earned $47 million. So a lawyer might earn 350,000, and depending on the performer, they might earn 80,000. But if you combine them, you'll get something new. And what you should combine are things that are essential to you. Not to other people, not something that's imitated. Because if Judge Judy imitated, she wouldn't be Judge Judy.

Fred Astaire, he was a historic dancer and if you've seen any of his films, you know he's an amazing dancer. But why did he stand out then? It's because he combined his ability to present and hold an audience that he gained from theater and he used it to dance in a different way. At that time, dancing was very formal and structured, but he did it in a loose, almost like a conversational style of dancing. And that's what made him a standout star. By combining, let's say an unusual past in a new industry, made him a star.

Karyn Mullen:

Now let's look at today, a maybe more approachable example. We've got a lot of e-marketing companies. So right now I like to sell products, and particular products and services that are tangible. That's just my preference. So right now everybody is saying, "Hey, I need to get online." And all the e-marketers are loving it right now. But when this moment passes and we all go back to work, if I was an e-marketer, I would start to market myself. This is one of the brands that I'm going to be building. Carmen's One-Step, it's a flooring adhesive. Now the thing is, why it would be a breakthrough would be, it's not used in a traditional, let's say product environment. So you use the same techniques that you use to sell online courses and you apply it to a physical product. As in terms of a career, you have your own niche and the product also does very well because it's sold in a different way. You can afford to sell this product, a higher quality product at the same price, if you use different tools of delivery.

Karyn Mullen:

So if you're planning on looking the same, which most people do, even though you're not, you're not going to survive as well. But if you start to combine something that everybody expects, let's assume you're an accountant. Well, the accountant has to actually have an accounting background, but you can't be exactly the same. So you look at you, are you a caring person? You put accounting plus heart to create your own niche. I'll give you an example that I wrote for a family member actually. There might be typos, but here we go. And she's in this position. "Mike Tyson, the professional . . ." Oh, by the way, this was on her resume or her covering letter. She's a very young lady.

Karyn Mullen:

"Mike Tyson, the professional boxer said, 'Everyone has a plan until you get punched in the face.' Before my dad died, I would have told you that I'm happy just being in finance. But after, I can tell you that there is more to me and more to life than my ability to be an excellent financial strategist. I am that for sure, but I am also caring and tenacious beyond measure. I have an ability to communicate and create measurable performance. I now have a burning desire to use all of my hard skills and my soft skills, all of me, to create something special with a special group of people. This is what brings me to your door and this opportunity."

Karyn Mullen:

So if you look at a pile of papers of people applying in the finance department, they're going to look the same. But if you're talking to your audience, which might be a business owner, not the head of accounting, this might be more appealing. Or if you wanted to apply to do the finances for an educational system, they'd be looking for this kind of person. And if you are heart plus accounting, you're the only person for this job.

Karyn Mullen:

Now you're looking for opportunities by looking at things that stand out, things that don't fit together. This is what I do. So in August I noticed, I love fashion, so I noticed at a high-end store that their clients were already coming in with face masks. Now that's just a thing. I noticed that it didn't match with the outfits. So if the outfits that they buy are three, sometimes to $15,000, I know big numbers, but then they had like a little paper face mask on. It was in congruent. It stuck out. They didn't fit together. At the time I said to my friends, maybe we should sell designer face masks. At that time, it wasn't going to be a runaway idea, but ideas are the source of your future wealth. Well, they contacted me after and they said, "We should have said yes to those masks," but of course that's the hindsight.

Karyn Mullen:

So this is what I had in my mind. Now we have another opportunity. I'm not saying this is a runaway success, but ideas, if you just keep generating ideas and ideas and ideas, you just need one and to stick to it, to make something happen. So you take gloves right now, you got vinyl gloves. You have the same audience. They're going to want cute gloves like the old Dior days. I know that I would. I asked a local seamstress to mock one up and I was going to put her in touch with my contacts. So it's not that I want you to come up with this example. I want you to come up with things that you see in your life that just stick out, that aren't congruent with the whole picture that could be.

Karyn Mullen:

Another way of creating is to connect, so to join together. This way is something very simple for you to do. Just turn on that switch that says, I'm looking for connections so you can help your friends and your neighbors and your family. And I didn't put your employer in here, or if you're a small business owner, your clients, but you are the thing that turns the others in the direction of their dreams. Social distancing might be here to stay, but you don't have to be distant from people. What people need right now, despite appearances, is you, your heart, your connection.

So this is a cover of my magazine. And although it is not part of how I grow businesses by double-digits, there is a connection because it's still, essentially how I grow them. So if you look at this cover model, she is a former Swimsuit Illustrated model. She's been on the cover of Vogue. Her name is Lana Ogilvie, and I should give credit to Jackie Gideon who did the creative direction and all the beauty here. And what I do is I kind of create a physical representation of the world I'm trying to create, the clients I'm trying to attract. I want jewelry clients, beauty clients, women that want more for themselves, I like clothes. I also have architecture. And building something physical so people can understand what I'm trying to create. And I want to show you what I mean by connect.

Karyn Mullen:

So Lana has her own jewelry line. You can see her Sabre Cuff on here. She also has her own skincare line. She's a model. However, she's more than just a model. So I have an article about her that shows all about her skincare line, all about her other talents, because I know that she would like to go back to being a talk show host or a presenter. So I included that, so somebody reading it, who has that opportunity can match her. So I'm helping her connect.

Karyn Mullen:

If you look at your neighborhood . . . Oopsie, Oh my goodness. Here we go.

So you look at your neighborhood or I look at my neighborhood, I see that there's a butcher down the street. I see there's a coffee shop and I see a bakery, but I see they do not help each other. The butcher can sell the coffee, like bags of ground coffee in his shop. The bakery, I mean, coffee and the baked goods go together. They could collaborate. But right now they order from somebody else semi-mediocre things, but if they combined really like boutique businesses, then they could help each other survive in the same way that you can help your friends survive and do well. They should be cross-promoting.

Karyn Mullen:

So then we look at a jewelry designer. I'm working with somebody right now. She loves the ocean. She does jewelry inspired by the ocean, but she's in landlocked Canada. So my job is to connect her amazing jewelry to people who live by the ocean and have retail stores. So right now she doesn't know that she has the problem, but I see that there's an opportunity and I'm connecting her with other people that can help her. But the point is you, or me in this case, can see the opportunity that they can't see. She doesn't think selling stuff about the ocean is a problem in the middle of Canada. And it's not because her work is gorgeous. However, she can make more money if we connect.

I'm running out of time, so I'm going to just say that your country, wherever you're from also has a brand. If you connect your product in a way that works with your country and how people think of your country, it's good for you. It makes you bigger. So if I sell anything related to nature or warmth, anything from Canada that relates to the cold, because that's how people think of Canada, it will do well. So if I had a health, let's say a nature bar or a granola product, that would do well as a Canadian product.

Karyn Mullen:

We have no time for this. I also have a friend who is from Puerto Rico. It's a US territory. He's a real estate developer and he gets investment from other people in Puerto Rico. However, it doesn't take advantage of the opportunity that he has across his border. So if he sold to Canadians, for example, you can invest in a real estate project and have an entire home basically for a $100,000 US in Puerto Rico. A Canadian is shocked by that. So we might have people who are interested in real estate in Canada, but there's no way we can get into it because the average house would be 600,000. So if he's fishing in the, let's say Puerto Rico pond, it's harder to catch fish. If he fishes in the Canadian pond where it looks so inexpensive, he'll do well. And the same with Canadians selling across the US border. It's in a way an imaginary border because we're trade friends. A $100,000 in the US equals 140,000 Canadian Dollars. So if you have 10 customers in Canada and 10 in the US, you'll make more money from your 10 US clients.

Karyn Mullen:

Now, this is the biggest, let's say, tip for you. Notice that organizations require three people for expansion. You need administration, somebody to take care of your legal and accounting. You need somebody to do sales and marketing, and you need somebody to deliver a great product. So this lone wolf thing, it's a sign of somebody who's struggling or tired. The second they're tired, their business collapses because they need to rest eventually. Your husband or your wife is part of that partnership and if you don't recognize them as an ally, you won't be able to benefit from it.

Karyn Mullen:

And here's an example of people I know. Lisa and Jason, they just recently got married. He had an IT tech relocation service. So when you move corporations . . . Oops, that's me telling I got very little time left.

Karyn Mullen:

When you move corporations, his company comes in and it disconnects computer and connects it at the new location. But here we enter, Lisa. His wife ran a very large camp. So she is so good at screening and security. She makes sure that everybody that works for them passes every level of criminal check possible. Together, they have the opportunity to create a new category, and that would be Secure iTech Moving, because IT moving. Because she's so good at administration and screening and he's so good at product delivery and moving and setting up technology that together that's unbeatable.

Karyn Mullen:

So you go around the world and you find organizations that are missing sections. If you're a first level employee, you look from zero to three months. If you're at the top, you might plan out for a year. But if you're the big boss and you don't have anybody in between; you're running around crazy in the day-to-day business. So maybe you're a level two that could help somebody and make their life more sane. You can help an owner have a much higher quality of life.

Karyn Mullen:

And I can invite my husband in right now. Honey! Honey!

It's also that you could translate between different departments. I've used different languages here. I've used English and French. However, it could be that you translate very well between management and IT techs. So whatever your gift is, is something you should market. You don't need more. You just need to market what you've already got.

And I always believe in coaching, no matter what. I don't care how much money you earn. For me, I will not do without my coaches and I don't just have one. I have coaches in different areas of my life, including my wonderful husband. And I think I better stop there unless . . . He's not that far away, but he's taking his time. Okay, I'll just keep going. Ideas-

Raymond Aaron:

I'm here.

Karyn Mullen:

Oh, that's how you're going to do it. Okay. Do you want to ask questions or do you want me to keep going, hon?

Raymond Aaron:

Well, I want to say that somebody got the idea of having matching face masks. They've created a new word, instead of bikini it's trikini. It's bottoms, tops and a face mask.

Karyn Mullen:

I do know that.

Raymond Aaron:

Yeah.

Karyn Mullen:

But see, that to me is . . . I hear you and I know you're joking, but the thing is, that's a reaction. So now everybody has it. But at the time that I said the idea, nobody had it.

Raymond Aaron:

Right.

Karyn Mullen:

> If you do it in advance, you're ready. You're not responding. Now you're like number one, you're ready to go.

Raymond Aaron:

> Karyn has let you in on the inside of some of the magical ways, at least it seems magical where things just change. Negative sales getting positive, companies start making money instead of losing money, companies that have been limping along, suddenly increase in their revenue and decrease in their costs. She's just a real magician in that regard. And I remember one day I was walking by her office and she was having a board meeting with all these big shot men in three-piece suits. And she was slamming her hand down on the boardroom table and they were quivering. My little petite wife weighs a 100 pounds and all these big guys at 150 to 200 pounds were quivering. Really, she's amazing. She's really, really amazing. And if you want to connect with her, then the best way to do it is on Instagram at @firstladyglobalmagazine. @firstladyglobalmagazine on Instagram.

Karyn Mullen:

> Raymond, can I just say one thing before we go here, because ideas not linked to your own personal gain, also, aren't very inspiring. But for example, a salesperson, let's say they have a sales target of $1 million. Well, okay, that's how a salesperson can increase their income. They can get to their goal and get paid. But somebody in finance can save 250,000, which in some corporations is equivalent to selling $1 million. If you went to your boss now, and you started while we're not at work, and you said, "Give me 10% of everything I saved this year," you know what, they're inclined to say yes.

Or if you wanted a job very badly and you wanted to start without getting any pay, you get paid out a result, you can start right away.

Raymond Aaron:

I love how creative you are, sweetheart. And you're the only speaker I can call sweetheart.

Karyn Mullen:

Well, you might call others sweetheart. Actually, you call a lot of people's sweetheart. You're fine.

Raymond Aaron:

But you're the only one I mean it to.

Karyn Mullen:

Okay, Bebe.

Raymond Aaron:

So I know you've been nervous for a couple of days, but you pulled it-

Karyn Mullen:

Well, I've done 700 slides. I have ideas on how to . . .

Raymond Aaron:

Thank you. You did a great job. You're wonderful. So to connect-

Karyn Mullen:

My intention was to help, but let's see if that worked. Yeah.

Raymond Aaron:

Yes. I already acknowledged you did a great job. You can connect with Karyn @firstladyglobalmagazine on Instagram. @ firstladyglobalmagazine on Instagram. And if you want Jack-

Being Up in Down Times

Paul O'Mahony

Raymond Aaron:

Paul, you are the United Kingdom's top internet marketer. And I am so proud of you, because I have decided to become an internet marketer. And yours is the product that I purchased. The relationship between the gigantic benefits that you deliver versus your very low price, I couldn't resist it. I bought it. I'm studying it, and I love it. And I want to share what I'm learning. Me, I bought your product. I want to share what I'm learning with my viewers. We have thousands of viewers from around the world. We broke GoToWebinar they couldn't handle us. We've had to spread out onto Facebook, on several Facebook groups and also YouTube Live. It's amazing. This is the biggest thing I've ever done online. I'm glad you're part of it. So go, tell us your wisdom.

Paul O'Mahony:

Yeah, so proud to be here. Thank you, Raymond. And it's very humbling to see the list of speakers that have been listening to, even Jack that was just on before Karen. And I have a signed copy of his book that he gave me a couple years ago. So very privileged to be here. What I would say to people right now is what this is about, just in case you're thinking, "Yeah, maybe I'll take a break. I've never heard of this guy before." I appreciate that. I understand that. However, I want to give you the practical guide as to what you can do in terms of turning things around from a financial perspective. The step by step guide of what you can do to take advantage of the opportunities that are sitting in front of us right now that most of us are not appreciating.

Paul O'Mahony:

And a lot of it is around the whole idea of social media. We'll be asking you some questions as we go through this. So feel free to type into the chat when I ask those questions. Like for example, how many of you right now think it is difficult to make money on the internet? So please type it out into the chat. How many of you think it's difficult to make money on the internet? Type me if you think that is you.

Paul O'Mahony:

Now, I'm not going to wait around for the answers because I have a very good sense of what they usually are. And the answer is normally about 80% of people say, "Yeah, me, me, it's difficult to make money on the internet." And then I'm going to ask you the question, how many of you have bought something purchase something on the internet in the last week? And I'm going to guess that the answer to that question is equally, so 80% of you have bought something on the internet, purchased something on the internet in the last week.

Paul O'Mahony:

So the answer to the first question should have been actually, you are really good at making money in the internet already, just for somebody else. You're amazing at making money on the internet, it's just the money is going from you to somebody else. What I want to show you is how do you switch that around? How do you turn that around and stop wasting time on social media and start making money from it. Because, you've heard it a million times in the news even in the last couple of weeks, about unprecedented times.

Paul O'Mahony:

But I'm not specifically talking about what's happening in the economy right now. I want to talk to you about what's happening with technology right now. This device, the smartphone, for the first time on the planet, there are now more phones on the planet than people. When people talk about once in a lifetime opportunities, this is way too overused, because the planet can only be connected once for the first time. And that has just happened. People are now connected all over the world.

Paul O'Mahony:

Now your device may not be [pleasured 00:03:30] in gold like this example, but it should be worth its weight in gold to you, and let me tell you why. The reason it should be worth its weight in gold to you is because quite simply, this is the biggest opportunity that has ever existed. Because right now people are addicted to these devices. What device wakes us up in the morning? Now a child is not a device, your phone wakes you up in the morning. What do you carry around with you all day, your phone in your handbag and that's just the men. What do we bring her up into the smallest room in the house or bathroom where nobody else's invited? Our phones. And what is our new routine at nighttime that we've learned since we were children to go down on our knees at nighttime by the side of our bed, but many of us are not praying anymore, we're kneeling down to plug in and charge our phones. This is the new world that we live in. We couldn't care less if our partner is charged in the morning. But if our phone starts off at a 12% battery in the morning, we know it's not going to be a good day.

Paul O'Mahony:

So I want to show you how you move away from being constantly being battered by messages and beeps and vibrations all day long, when it's somebody else looking for your time to focus your energy and ultimately your money. So how do you use that instead of it being a liability and taking money out of your pocket, to turn it into the biggest asset in your life to put money into your pocket. So regardless of whether you own your own business, regardless of whether you want to be an influencer and you have a book or a brand or you're about to finish writing a book. Or if you hate social media, and you're very, very nervous about publicly expressing your opinions or putting your own face out there, it absolutely doesn't matter. This still applies to you, we must engage with social media because there's over three and a half billion people on it, half of the planet.

Paul O'Mahony:

So if we decide to leave that alone, we're missing out on the biggest opportunity that is out there right now. And that is being able to engage with people in the platforms that they enjoy.

Now, I wanted to talk to you a little bit about myself before I delve any deeper into this. I'm very lucky in that 10 years ago, I was introduced to a workshop, a three-day workshop in Ireland actually where I'm from, in case you haven't picked up on that. In 2009, February 2009. And in case . . . I don't know if there's any of you Irish people out there, but we're extremely skeptical.

Really, really skeptical. And if you don't believe our skeptical, it doesn't matter, we don't believe you anyway, we don't believe people. We don't take them at their word.

Paul O'Mahony:

But I have a picture at me at this very first conference that I went to, when there were multiple speakers all talking about how they were making millions on the internet. I'm sorry, that's the wrong picture. Here we go. That's a different event later tonight. Here we go. So this is a picture of me, nine years into my corporate job when I called in sick for the first time in nine years borrowed my work laptop, which I actually must get back. And I obviously got a little bit like a rabbit in the headlights because I was seeing all these guys talking about how they were making millions on the internet. And I just couldn't believe it. I said, "This has got to be a scam." So I talked to the person next to me and said, "This is a scam. Right?" They said, "Of course it's a scam because if it was this easy, everybody else will be doing it." I said, "Yeah, that sounds right. I've heard that one before."

Paul O'Mahony:

But what I actually decided to do was after listening to multiple speakers talking about and proving the fact that they have got a completely different financial set of affairs and I was heading off the path of, I decided to invest in three separate programs and from three complete strangers to me before that weekend. And decided what's the worst that can happen here? What's the worst that can happen? But the worst that can happen is that I don't follow this. Is that I don't use this. But it doesn't depend on the economy going up or down. It doesn't depend on the property market going up or down. I've got an education, to learn how to sell anything to anybody 24 hours a day, seven days a week. And regardless of what happens around the world, I can always solve people's problems because that's ultimately what serves people financially. Is help others solve their problems, and ultimately, that will solve yours.

Paul O'Mahony:

Now, this is totally where I started from the internet is a scam, but I'll never forget what one speaker said. He picked up on the fact how skeptical we were. One guy told us to point to the person next to us and tell them they're awesome. Now we're Irish. We don't do that.

Paul O'Mahony:

Another guy came in and he said, stand up and massage the shoulders of the person next to you. Long before social distancing was a thing or before it was a popular, we naturally do that in Ireland. We don't even hold our own families. We don't drink because we enjoy it, we drink because we need to procreate. But he was totally [inaudible 00:08:20] sort of thing. But at the same time, this guy came in and he said, "You think you're so smart," he said, "You're looking at all this and you think we're here to brainwash you." But he said, "Ironically, you are actually already brainwashed. You believe that your wealth is connected to the education system, to the number of letters you get after your name. To the qualifications that you get in your first 20 years of life." He said, "I have found as a high school dropout, that I'm better measure of wealth rather than being the number of letters after your name like BSC, or BA or MSC or MA or PhD. He said its actually numbers in your bank account.

Paul O'Mahony:

And I remember when I heard that and I said, "I don't like this guy." I didn't like him to begin with, now I definitely don't like him. Because sometimes when you hear the truth, it really, really hurts. Now, both my teachers are . . . both my parents should I say are teachers, so my entire life was about you need to go to school, college, do well in your exams, work for 50 years and get yourself a pensionable job or a permanent job. If you remember those permanent jobs that were all the rage about 10 years ago, and it just turned out not to be so permanent. But at the same time, it was very much going against the grain for me, I was definitely not following the plan that parents, friends, family had outlined that this is the way towards wealth. And you know what, he pointed it out, and I realized he was correct.

Paul O'Mahony:

As he said, professors and universities don't drive to college in Lamborghinis, they cycle on bicycles. And I remember when he said that, I said, "That's actually quite true." And he said, your wealth may be up here, but it doesn't mean it's going to be in your bank account. So from that day, I understood what Mark Twain meant when he said never . . . He said, "I never let my schooling get in the way of my education." And so many people think they know what that means, but I truly believe you need this sort of shock to the system to actually understand what that means.

Paul O'Mahony:

So at that event, everything completely changed. As I said, I invested in three products, I didn't even bring my credit card with me the first day that will show you how naive I was to this entire thing. But every day, I am so grateful that I made that decision, not to listen to the people around me, but just to actually listen to the people who had the results in my life, not comparing, why aren't other people doing this, especially when they don't have the resources that I'm hoping to achieve in my life.

Paul O'Mahony:

So I want to if you don't mind to type into the chat a huge thank you to Raymond, to Wendy, to Mikey to Karen and to everybody who's had a part in putting this together over the past month or so. And of course, the amazing speakers that have been here, because you are in the same position as me virtually admittedly, but at the end of the day you can make a decision that today is the tipping point. There's no more looking back, everything's going to change. And it starts today. In fact, I will invite you right now to pick up your phone, take a selfie of you, looking at me, looking at you, looking at Raymond, so that you have this on your phone in your favorites to say, this was the day April 25th 2020, when I finally got 2020 vision about what I want to do. And I took control and ownership of where my finances are going to be.

Paul O'Mahony:

And rather than relying on what happens in the external world and the external economy, we're looking within to see what can we do to take ownership of what are the key practical steps that you can follow starting today to change the whole thing around in your favor.

Now every good story has to relate back to Tony Robbins at some point or another. So I certainly have mine, because when I went to the three events about paid for back in our event in 2009, this guy's name kept coming up over and over again. Tony Robbins, Tony Robbins. So I convinced my boss that I would like to go see Tony Robbins in New York City on St. Patrick's weekend of all weekends, 2009. And he was a great boss, he paid for it. He was working on my leadership skills. And I remember thinking, "Well, this is going to be amazing. How could this possibly go wrong?" But interestingly enough, I'd never seen Tony before, I hadn't even checked him out on YouTube. But he came out on stage and the place went crazy. There was only 3,000 people there, which seems like a small crowd nowadays when we have the same amount registered for this. But back then that was a huge crowd in New Jersey in Secaucus. And it was like Kanye West, the Pope and Kim Kardashian were all combined into one person because the place went mental.

Paul O'Mahony:

And Tony comes out and as he says, in his nice polite way, he said, "Everybody, I want you to jump around like complete lunatics." And to my absolute shock and horror, that was all it took. 2995 people started jumping around like complete lunatics. I started backing off to the closest exit. I bumped into a guy . . . you could not make this up. He had ginger hair and freckles. He couldn't have looked more Irish. He looked at me. He was about to say something, I said, "Before you say anything, I just want you to know, I did not use my money to be here." He said, "Forget the money. I've already written it off. This is a cult, I've seen on the Discovery Channel. Now I know how we walk on fire and survive. We're going to drink suicide tablets, and they're going to drag us across the coals to get rid of the evidence." He said, "Let's just go for a drink at St. Patrick's weekend." And I remember thinking, "You know what, you're probably right." We weren't by ourselves, by the way. There was two Germans there as well going, "What is this?" So there was the Irish and the Germans. And then Tony says, "Oh, by the way, those of you not dancing. You're walking on fire tonight. If you don't do everything I say, you're going to burn."

Paul O'Mahony:

And I thought about it for a second, In said, "Okay, Tony, why don't we just say so all I needed was a bit of motivation." And off I went jumping around the crowd, this is from the official website with me jumping up and down a couple of hours later saying, "Touch me, Tony, please touch me." And we touched. He touched me in places that . . . actually I can't say that anymore. We had a connection that I just thought was different to other people. I couldn't quite put my finger on what it was. My leprosy was instantly cured. It was definitely gods that I was are dealing with.

Paul O'Mahony:

So I texted my boss, I quit my job, and my plan was going to fake it till you make it, and live with passion. What I decided to do was to ignore the real advice that Tony gave, which was now that you're enthusiastic, now that you're active and you're charged and you're ready to take action, get yourself a coach. Pay for a coach, find a system that works that will get you to where you want to go. And I said "Yeah, I'm not so sure I like that, I don't normally like that, but it sounds a bit salesy."

Paul O'Mahony:

So what did I try and do? I tried to master the stock market by myself. Three months later, I lost all the money I had saved from nine years in my job, because I would not pay a coach for help. My ego got in the way once more. So that was when July 2009. I resorted back to the internet because it costs nothing to get going. I have no other choices. And the last thing I wanted to do was to go back to work with my tail between my legs. And that's when everything changed for me. Started with Twitter then moved into different social networks. Now I get to speak to hundreds of thousands of people per year. Every year we get to share the stage with the likes of Raymond, Jack, John Assaraf is one of my good friends, and multiple speakers that are actually on over the next couple of days, and Mark Victor Hansen. And these guys that I looked up to so much as speakers from that secret all those years ago, not realizing that the secret was taking ownership, taking responsibility. Stop pointing fingers at everybody else because there's three fingers pointing back at you, but the difference is, we have never had the opportunity for the entire time that humanity has been on the planet to get so wealthy so quick by using the technology that exists today.

Paul O'Mahony:

In 10 years from now, people will look back at the time when the entire world was addicted to smartphones, and nobody realizes they're addicted. And they'll say, "Oh my God, back then you didn't even need a license to have a phone. You could just decide to sell a business. You could just sell all their businesses products, nobody even cared, you could do whatever you liked. In fact, it costs a dollar to run an ad on Facebook, it cost a cent to run an ad on Twitter." And the other person will look at them like they're crazy and say, "No, it wasn't because if it was like that. Everybody would have been doing it." Guess what, that is exactly where we are right now. Except with Corona, with the horrendous thing that's happening right around the world right now, you actually could not be starting in a better time because ads are on sale right now.

Paul O'Mahony:

You have just been given the biggest gift that has been handed out within business, the business world for the last five years, because ads are on sale. Because the minute that people panic, businesses and entrepreneurs do exactly the opposite of what they should do. They cut down their ad spend.

Paul O'Mahony:

Imagine, when you need more clients, the first thing they do is they stop paying to acquire clients. But that's what happens when you don't get advice from coaches or mentors who have been there and done that. That's what happened when you learn your business skills in college, rather than from people who actually do it practically. Would you get into a car with somebody, a vehicle, who has just passed a theory exam, but they've never practically driven a car? That's what college is like nowadays, you get a degree in how to run a business that you've never practically ran on.

Paul O'Mahony:

So we got to figure out how do we go from the craziness of today's world where there's a 96% chance of a business failing, traditional business, to a 99% chance of having success with the business if you follow the system. So I want to be sharing with you today.

Now you get to meet amazing people. Lots of them actually I want to be chatting to them over the next couple of days. This is Jack Dorsey the founder of Twitter. When we met, we were making more money from Twitter than he was which was interesting. Robert Kiyosaki, John Assaraf. Tony, of course, when we met a couple of times, after our initial meeting in '09.

Paul O'Mahony:

Ladies, you've already spotted this. But guys, in case you haven't, look at the size of his hand, it's the size of my entire chest. Let's just say that was a sign for me never to compete in his niche of having long term, passionate relationships. Long term, long being the key word there. Not to say the first time I spoke to Tony on stage back about four or five years ago now, I did my best to photoshop . . . to bring my hand off [inaudible 00:18:40] kind of sizes, but still, it just didn't quite get there.

Paul O'Mahony:

But saying that within a year of starting out, myself and my business partner, we made our first million dollars with zero experience on the internet, zero experience to social media. I'm not technical. Believe me when I say that. I am not technical. Genuinely it's not something I'm strong in, and the thing is, you don't need to be. If you did, every IT manager in the world would be a millionaire. But it's not about technical knowledge. It's just knowing about how to apply it. Or as I say to people, the difference between you and somebody making millions on the internet is simply this, the sequence of the keys that you press on your keyboard. You just got to press the buttons in a different order, the keys in a different order. And if I can press your buttons to get you to press those buttons, we are onto a winning formula between us all.

Paul O'Mahony:

Fortunately, I've had many awards from what we do in terms of our business. I've a Guinness World Record for speaking, and my brand is Rethink, where I give people the tools to think differently so that they can get different results in their life, to empower people to lead extraordinary lives. I've written books about social media, Rethink Time Management, I have a huge focus on children and teenagers around money. I've written the book of Raymond as well which we'll be launching hopefully later this year. And I've a company and a foundation helping children and teenagers called FUNancial Freedom.

Where I've invested over half a million into animation to teach children from seven up to 19 years of age teenagers how to become empowered around money, business, giving back, what money can do, in terms of not just getting something but also giving back and making an impact on the planet and helping the less well off.

Paul O'Mahony:

So this is where I'm at and that we're planning on having five million children through this in the next couple of years. But it's extremely inspiring what you can do when you embrace these technologies, rather than being afraid of them because they are a reality. We are the last ever generation that will have rang a building when you're looking for somebody rather than ringing a person. So we really are a relic of the past. And we need to move on if we do want to engage with the world that we're in today from an economics and a finances' perspective. Because children get it.

This guy Salman, for example, came to my workshop with his dad because the babysitter canceled on them last minute. And he put up his hand and said, "Paul, I've just made $210." I remember saying, "Salman, how long did that take?" He said, "11 minutes." Every adult in the room had the same look on their face, like, you little S-H-I-T. You can imagine what they said, right? Because they could not believe that this was possible, because as an adult, we're constantly looking for reasons why something won't work. While as a child, all you need is just one opportunity, and to go and do that.

Paul O'Mahony:

So we launched that last May in Johannesburg, our first event had 55,000 children added Johannesburg. We gave more free copies of a book behind my head here to rethink money for children and teens. And it's truly inspiring to be able to change an entire generation. And I hope that you start to feel inspired and feel motivated to pick up wherever you are right now and say you know what, I'm just not playing at the level I should be at. There are things I can do that much higher level, but I just need to step up and do that. And here are speaking of steps, the four-step process that you need to follow.

Paul O'Mahony:

The first is this, you want to pick a niche or a niche where people have problems consistently, don't overthink it. Especially my perfectionist friends, I used to have that perfectionist myself. Especially you guys do not overthink what you're about to get into. It's way more important that you just get started, get the money coming in, understand how it works, and then you can scale it, and you can expand it out. Once we know what niche we're in, then we go to social media, we find the people with the problem that we want to help solve that problem. Then we go to our Opt-in page our squeeze page, it's sometimes called.

Paul O'Mahony:

Now you have to fill out one of these to be here today. This is not uncommon to anybody anymore. They know exactly what it is, in order to get a free gift of some form, you give your contact details. And then you finally, you automate the process of making money by selling either your own products, your own services, or somebody else's products or somebody else's services. So when it comes to choosing your niche, I suggest you stick with what Zig Ziglar says. "You can have everything in life you want, if you will just help enough other people get what they want." That is absolutely critical to being successful in business and understanding marketing. Find out what the client wants and give it to them.

Paul O'Mahony:

What your clients want, all over the world consistently, regardless of whether it was before COVID, post COVID, during COVID, they want to be healthier, they want to be wealthier, they want to be happier. Those are the three biggies, I would never even go too far from there whatsoever. Whatever product you're selling connect it to one of the these. In fact, stop even thinking about products because people don't buy products for the sake of products. They're buying products because they want the solution and benefit and outcome.

Paul O'Mahony:

So focus on one of these areas because there are already hundreds of thousands of products that exist. There are millions of web pages that you could sign up to sell the best products in the world for free. You don't even need to create these yourself. So it will allow you to relax from a sense of worrying about what happens if my product goes out of date? It will. What happens if somebody comes in with a better product? They will. What happens if somebody comes in and undercuts me? They will. So all of these certainties we need to handle and deal with.

Paul O'Mahony:

And we do that by getting into areas where there will be an endless supply of products that you can promote forevermore by focusing and learning one skill, which we will call the skill of matchmaking. And that's why we use social media because social media gives us the platform to get in front of the perfect people that we want. And in the world that we live in today, where we're constantly being bombarded by the media telling us that everything is going crazy, everything is not good. The world keeps on changing and whatever you know right now it's going to change. It's extremely difficult to have any certainty. It's extremely difficult, should I say, to feel confident about your children's future.

Paul O'Mahony:

And I would say the same if you're about to set up a business to start off in the business. If you're being told that everything you know is going to change, that's not exactly going to fill you with confidence until now. Because this is why I choose this vehicle for making money over any other vehicle, whether that be property, whether that be the stock market, whether that be a traditional business, I choose this business. Because it's not based on anything that's going to change. In fact, that's based on two key foundation stones that will never change.

Paul O'Mahony:

Now, that's a big claim to make, I appreciate. But the reason I'm telling you this is because I 100% believe this and you will adjust to moments when I explain it to you. The first thing that will never change is this, people will never stop having problems. That is a given. One, let's say two months ago, we were in the height of a bull market, nine years the second longest bull market in history, everybody's excited, up, up, up. Two months later, we're on the way down. We're on the way down. We haven't quite got there yet. But still people continue to have problems. The problems have just changed form. So, that will never stop.

Paul O'Mahony:

So that's the person on the left hand side, the green jigsaw puzzle. They're a regular person with regular problems. So we want to deal in certainties. So we're going to deal in that certainty. People will always have problems.

Paul O'Mahony:

On the right hand side, the person with the blue jigsaw puzzle is an entrepreneur, an entrepreneur as Lori Greiner, the lady who was covered . . . her story was covered in the movie Joy, a couple of years ago, the lady who invented the squeezy mop. I love her quotation about entrepreneurs where she says, entrepreneurs are the only people I know who work 80 hours a week, to avoid a 40 hour a week job. And if you're an entrepreneur right now, you know you're chuckling. But it's not exactly funny because it's so true that it hurts. 85% chance of a solopreneur going out of business in year one, of the 15% that survived, there's an 85% chance of those 15% and they will go out of business in year two. These are people who are smart, they're clever. They're graduates of universities, some of them have MBAs, they've got business degrees yet somehow, they manage to have a 96% to 98% chance of failure. Why? Because we are learning how to run a business from people who never run a business. And if they did run a business, they ran a business 10 years ago, 20 years ago, 30 years ago, the game has changed, the world has changed.

Paul O'Mahony:

Look at the companies that are going bankrupt looking for declaring bankruptcy in the last two weeks. Some of the biggest household names that we know in business because they haven't adapted . . . they haven't moved online. And if you have a company, that the doors can be shut down physically, your finances can be shut down at any time point in time.

Paul O'Mahony:

So we have to move away from that, instead of a 96% chance of failure, I want to show you to have a 99% chance of success by being the matchmaker. Learning how to find the people with the problem and introduce them to the best products that exist. And before you even get a chance to say "Well, Paul, if it was that easy, wouldn't everybody else be doing that?" Forget about everybody else. Let's look at some of the most successful companies in the world like Uber, the world's largest taxi company, doesn't own any vehicles. Facebook, the world's largest content sharer, doesn't create any content. Alibaba, the world's largest store, doesn't have any inventory. Airbnb, the world's largest accommodation provider doesn't own any real estate. Booking.com, Trivago.com, Hotels.com they don't own any hotels. Amazon.com doesn't create or write a single book. eBay doesn't create a single product. Banks have been doing this for centuries where to take money off one person and then sell it to the next person in the line. This is how the most successful companies in the world work today. They don't take the risk of traditional business, they become the matchmaker. If it's good enough for them, it's obviously more than good enough for us. But the thing is, sometimes it's so close to us that we don't see the wood from the trees.

Paul O'Mahony:

So we now live in a world where we are connected to people all day, every day and we can sell the best selling products on the planet as our own, get people to sign up for free as a partner or an affiliate and get paid commission to just let other people book their holidays on Booking.com. Or for you to purchase something on Amazon and you get paid every time you buy something. The reason you're not doing this is because the people you're surrounded with don't do it. But I'm telling you, there are plenty of people out there that are doing this every single day. And in fact, you will save more in the next few months with your spending habits than you'll ever invest in me in terms of teaching you how to do that.

Paul O'Mahony:

So you will save 10, 20 to 30 times what you would invest in me just from a savings' perspective even before you even think about making money which is pretty incredible claim if you think about it. Now I want to share something with you here that I want to really bring into focus how bad the problem is and why we need to get charged up and do something about it. Especially in the world right now when we're hearing about the rescue packages that are $2 trillion, and another 600 billion [inaudible 00:30:01] on top of that. We forget how big a trillion is. A million seconds is 12 days, a billion seconds is 33 years. A trillion seconds is 33,000 years. Hopefully that gives you a perspective between a million dollars and a trillion dollars.

Paul O'Mahony:

Because if you take a trillion dollars and you add another 600 billion to it, you get this big number $1.6 trillion, which is the number one US government's asset on their books. What is it? Outstanding student loan debt. You heard me right, outstanding student loan debt. The average graduate in the US has to pay back a loan of $37,000. The only loan you can never declare bankruptcy on is a student loan. The average person in the US spends $600,000 in a lifetime on interest on debt alone.

Paul O'Mahony:

We are following a system that instead of allowing us to become financially free, it sends us down in the spiral of debt constantly. And we're to blame the parents, the nephews and nieces, the neighbors. Because what do we tell our children to do once they graduate from college, we then say, "Get yourself a house, go on, you and your partner and get yourself a house." Or another word for this mortgage coming from the word [more tear 00:31:18], more tear comes from the Latin word to die. Mortgage actually means debt until death. Obviously, mortgage sounds a lot better when you're selling it. But that's what mortgage means, "Hey, get some debt until death."

Paul O'Mahony:

So we are trying to fast track our kids into this spiraling debt problem. It never made sense to me that a three-year-old is better off financially than a 23-year-old. But if enough people do it, nobody declares us insane, if enough people do it, we say it's normal. However, that's why I'm here today to just get you to rethink about this, and how you can claim ownership of this. Turn this whole thing around by building yourself what's called a mailing list or an email list or a database where you can literally solve the problems of people. And your income is a direct outcome of the amount of people that you help, not the hours that you work.

Paul O'Mahony:

So you can take ownership, you can even slip away from the rat race. But more than anything, you decide how much you want to make. And then you go and do that, on average, per email address that you have in your niche, you should be making $1 per person on your list every single month. So if you want to be making an extra $5,000 a month, you immediately decide I am going to create a list of 5,000 people. If you want to make $10,000 a month, rather than focusing on the money where you're disempowered, you focus on what you can do, which is create a list 10,000 people and you go and do that. And that's what I want to be walking you through here now.

The objective of social media is not to do any selling is to invite people to come off of social media, which is a very cluttered environment, and into our database so that we know when we email them, it's sitting there for their inbox the next time they come back.

Paul O'Mahony:

So let's see for example, if we're trying to work out the calculations, if you're making $1 per person per month, which doesn't sound like a lot, but if it costs you $1 to get somebody's email address with a Facebook ad, and you made $1 per month, that's $12 per year, taking off the cost. You have a return on investment of 1100% per year from a dollar spend. And you might say, "So what good is a dollar, how can I spend the dollar?" Welcome to the world of Facebook, it's $1 to get started on Facebook today in 2020, and ads are on sale. I cannot tell you that often enough today because that is the best news you're going to hear all weekend.

Paul O'Mahony:

Ads are on sale, Facebook ads are on sale, YouTube ads are on sale, Twitter ads are on sale, Instagram ads are on sale. Jump in you have been given a lifeline that you can learn cheaply, quickly and you can catch up and not only catch up, you can escalate quickly and pass out businesses who are now feeling contractual, they're feeling down and in depth about what they're doing while you can be ascending, helping more and making more money by doing that.

Paul O'Mahony:

So as I said, social media is about building a list. And then it's about following up and making money from that specifically. And it shouldn't come as a surprise to people all over the world from as young as 11 years of age to 86 years young, can make this work. Raymond himself has just started on the program too because all we're doing is solving problems for people. If you don't have your own products, it doesn't matter.

Paul O'Mahony:

In fact, those of you that are interested in learning from me, we are going to be starting on Monday, and I will pick your niche for you. We don't leave anything up to question, anything up to debate, we just get going, get started, make it happen.

Paul O'Mahony:

Rune made $130 in four hours from following this system in just four single hours. That's US dollars. And I do run workshops back in the day when we used to have live events in person. I used to run them in the UK once every few months, and there are $6,000 to come through it, but they're all booked out with a massive backlog now obviously with what's just going on. But we'll come back to that little bit later before we finish here today.

Paul O'Mahony:

What's unique about the way I teach, however, is that I teach you long before you ever come to the workshop. I teach you immediately. We start on Monday, as I said already, we start Monday, actually noon, Eastern, so we can get stuck in straightaway. Because I do not want you to wait, given the environment we are in right now you have the greatest opportunity that has been for over a decade and possibly going back even further. But because right now, if you have an opportunity that people have not had or could not even have dreamt of just even six months ago.

Paul O'Mahony:

And Janet, for example, run her first Facebook ads turned $12 into $2,100 in 12 hours. And you know what she did? She panicked. She turned off her ad and said this can't be legal. It can't be legal to make money that fast. Alison 63 years of age has gone on to make over $12,000 a month and she said, "Paula Just think of it like a cookbook recipe. I knew the ingredients and I mixed them in the right way." She said, "If you do that, you could know the ingredients to bake a cake." She says, "And you could know, that it needs to go into an oven. But if you don't know the right amount to mix, and you don't know the temperature and the time to put them into the oven, it goes in a mess. And it comes out a mess." And she said, "That's how I was on the internet. I somehow used Google and Facebook and my computer to spend money rather than to make money." And she had three grandkids in her care, she was working double shifts in[inaudible 00:36:23] estate to fund her lifestyle. Suddenly, she had gone on to make over 12 grand a month from her online business.

Paul O'Mahony:

So that's what I want to share with you just follow the system follow the process. And the key thing you got to say to yourself is if somebody else can do this, then so can I. And if you have your phone with you take a picture of this because I do not have the chance today to get go into detail about what I cover in my workshops. But if it is something that already intrigues you or you're even a little curious about please take a picture of it so you do know what is encompassed within it. Everything that we teach in there all comes into the center point of view. Learning how do you turn this into money? You can learn about social media every day of the week. But I'm here to show you how do you turn that into income? How do you turn it into money specifically?

Paul O'Mahony:

So quick recap. You need to be in a niche where people have the problems already, make it easy for yourself, and that is much easier to find the people. Then we're going to build a database, then we're going to automate that process. And the last step is you need support, regardless of wherever you are right now, whether you're a complete beginner who hasn't even got a Facebook account, no problem. Or whether you're quite advanced like Raymond, who has a business for decades and still realizes, okay, there's so much more I can do on the internet. Support is always required to take you to the next level.

Paul O'Mahony:

Some of my clients that have heard of Booking.com, the world's largest spender with Google ads, Johnson & Johnson. When I started in 2009, 2010, my hourly fee was $32, $33. And remember my mentor saying to me back then, "Paul, you're so cheap." And now you understand what he means, because a decade later, my one to one mentoring is $100,000. And it's closed up for 19 months, is completely booked out. I allow two days a month per consultant, and that's it. Two young daughters, and priorities change when money is handled.

Paul O'Mahony:

But what I'm going to be saying to you is one other thing could you learn right now, that would allow you to add much more value to you, that you could add that much value to the market that people would be willing to learn and spend and invest that much money in you. I'm not saying you'll figure this out in 25 minutes. But what I am saying is, if you do decide to learn this, you are going to a whole new level of knowledge that will enable you to completely change your wealth moving forward.

Paul O'Mahony:

And this is why it works. This is why the whole thing works. People are very, very much trained to go to Google to type in a problem that they might have like, I want to lose weight. And what shows up? Websites selling them weight loss products. However, if you go to a website like Twitter, and I'm on a very limited time today, with the 55 minutes that I have, so I'm going to pick the social network that you would feel has the least possible opportunity to be good in business. I teach Instagram, I teach Facebook, we teach Pinterest, we teach is LinkedIn, we teach YouTube, we teach blogging, we teach all of those. But I want to convince you with the one you least expect, with Twitter.

Paul O'Mahony:

Because if you type into Twitter, the exact same statement that we had in Google there, I want to lose weight. Look at what happens. You get a list of people who have just said they have that problem. Not websites selling you a product. Linda . . . sorry, Carla says, "I want to lose weight." Short and to the point. Linda, "I'm watching the Meerkat Manor. I want the same metabolism as a meerkat. They lose 5% of their body weight overnight and need to eat lots." There you go in case, you thought you learn nothing off me today. Caitlin, "I only want two things, to lose weight and to eat." Denise, "I only want two things in life to lose weight and to eat." And if you scroll down, there are more, more and more people, "All I want in life is to lose weight and to gain money yet instead here I am gaining weight and losing money." "I'm trying to lose weight," says Elizabeth. "It's so hard. All I want is tacos, pizzas, burritos and chips." Jennifer says, "I want to lose weight, but I keep eating at midnight." And if you are with your friends looking at this, you would say to each other that is why I don't go near Twitter. It is full of mental people. And I don't disagree, everybody's mental.

Paul O'Mahony:

However, you are thinking as a consumer, you're not rethinking social media. You're not thinking as somebody who actually would appreciate that these people are crying out for help. They're willing to share their problem with 350 million strangers. Do you think they're likely to take action around this? Of course. Not them all, but lots of them will. Now you might say, "Well, Paul, I don't have a weight loss product." Who cares? Weight Watchers do, why not sign up to Weight Watchers for free and recommend Weight Watchers products to these people. They already love to know them at trust them. I've just given you little examples in time that we have today, to start to get your attention, I hope and maybe light a light bulb for you to think, "Hang on, I think I might have been doing things a little bit more difficult than I could have."

Paul O'Mahony:

My question would be if I was you is, am I a little bit late to the market? You could not be starting at a better time. Let's go back to our friend Tony we mentioned earlier. Three million followers on Twitter. What's that got to do with you? Everything. Because you can get your message in front of his followers. You do something called Twitter advertising, you can get clicks onto your Opt-in page. Or you can pay for conversions, which means you only pay when you collect an email address. Or if you're sending people to a sales page, like a Tony Robbins event, for example, if you had a sales page for that, you would only pay when somebody buys.

Paul O'Mahony:

Now, if you're a business owner, you think, "Hang on a second, that doesn't sound like business." In fact, that's what my accountant says. He said, "Oh, you don't teach business. You teach magic. You teach people how to acquire clients without taking any risk." I said, "I know." What do you think he started doing? He stopped paying being paid by the hour and he started selling digital products. He started recommending software's like Sage and Zero and Intuit to his clients and he gets paid a monthly commission because it's always very common or very . . . sorry, sensical when you see it, and it's very obvious. But most people just like the matchmaking exercise with Uber and Facebook and Booking.com et cetera. People are not doing it because they just do not see enough other people doing it. It's not common knowledge.

Paul O'Mahony:

Now what I'm going to show you here is so good at almost should be illegal. You can put your message in front of people based on the keywords that they use. So if you're helping people lose weight, you could put them in front of anybody that says anything like I need to lose weight, I want a six pack, how do I lose the belly or whatever it is. You can target people based on the television show that they're watching. You can target people based on who they have as followers.

Paul O'Mahony:

So Tony Robbins has three million followers, but will Twitter say well maybe that's not enough because we can get you his look alike followers people that are very similar to his, we've got 46 million of those. So just in case . . . this is why I'm saying to you this is the perfect time to start. You can leverage other people's work, and who's stuff do you think you would sell to his people? Not your stuff? I don't care who you are, you sell Tony's stuff to Tony's people. In case, you're thinking, "What? But what about me?" Forget about you. Do you want to build a bank account or do you want a bigger ego? Why don't you sell Tony Robbins' book to Tony Robbins' people, Jack Canfield's books to Jack Canfield's people. Why don't you sell . . . What is . . . Richard Branson books to people who follow Virgin, or Harry Potter books to people that follow J.K. Rowling.

Paul O'Mahony:

Now you might think but they won't like that. They will love that because you get paid, they get paid. You are making them sales that they would not have made themselves. We are overthinking if we're making business way too hard. And remember, this is Twitter, the one that I wouldn't even expect you to start with. But I want to break the mindset that people have that social media is for kids or teens or it doesn't work, or I tried Facebook ads, and it doesn't work. And I don't ever disagree with somebody on that, because I don't want another competitor, unless you're here training and learning from me.

But I say, Facebook, don't want to take your money. Facebook wants to work with you on a long-term basis before both of you make money. The more money you make, the more money they make.

Paul O'Mahony:

If your business isn't doing this, you are about to go out of business. And what I would say is, type in the chat right now if you think that I might be able to help you. Please type in, "Help me, Paul." "Help me Paul," if you think I could just help you a little bit with your business because I know I can. Now what if you just wanted to target wealthy people when you absolutely can on Twitter, for example? You can target people based on whether they own a home outright, or whether they rent a home or whether they're in the market to buy a home. You can target people on based on the past that they have. You can target people based on their credit history, their credit worthiness, excellent credit worthiness 11.6 million. This is just in the US alone, when you run over them another 6.2 million very good. You could target people based on their discretionary spending, how much spare money do they have? You can target people based on their net worth, you can cut straight to the chase. One million plus, one million to two million. Affluency, affluent parents 3.5 million.

Paul O'Mahony:

Ladies if you learn nothing else over this weekend, go straight to Twitter, affluent single men in the US 768,000, you can close down your accounts with. Who can you close your accounts down with? Swipe left, swipe right, Tinder, close them down. Forget it. Get straight onto Twitter, cut straight to the chase. And you can find exactly what needs to be found about anybody right in here. It's incredible, what's possible.

Paul O'Mahony:

The reason I'm just showing you the tip of the iceberg here is because I want you to rethink social media. But chances are you are not aware of this, you have no idea that you can target people based on credit cards they have, when they last received their credit card, what's the value of their home. And with Facebook, they make it so easy for people to leave their email addresses that they don't even ask people to put their name and email anymore. They say click a link once, they will automatically populate the name and email for you. So two clicks $1 per person, per month, 24 hours a day, seven days a week.

Paul O'Mahony:

As I said at the start, you either are the target or you do the targeting yourself. It's your choice. It's happening in front of you all of the time, but most people do not have the awareness to see what's happening. That ad by the way on Facebook is called Lead Generation.

Paul O'Mahony:

Now my Facebook and Twitter ads courses as I said with $1 to run a Facebook ad, it's incredible in 2020. One cent to run one on Twitter. I do have courses online you can find them for $4,000, £3000, or it's about four and a half thousand Canadian. But we'll come back to that in a little bit.

Paul O'Mahony:

Now, this doesn't even talk about the likes of Instagram. But the super sexy social networks that we have right now. Jake, for example, $26,000 in a single hour, he used to be a teacher in Manchester in the UK, he's given that up to obviously pursue this, because it makes no sense when you can make more than in an hour than you do with a year in your job.

Paul O'Mahony:

Vishal made $55,000 in three hours from using Facebook Messenger. Now you are probably familiar with this tool. But again, you're being used by it rather than using it to completely change your finances. And this the sample of people all over the world.

Paul O'Mahony:

Alfred works 60 hours a week as an anesthetist. He sends me a message saying, "Hey Paul just have another milestone today. $200 in a single day from sales." At the workshop, he was saying I'm making $350 per day. That's 127 grand per year for somebody in a full-time job 60 hours a week. I'm pretty sure that would probably take the pressure off for most people around the world.

Paul O'Mahony:

And the thing about all of this is exciting and all this it is, I want you to be grateful to for where you're starting from. Because you have such an opportunity with WiFi, with 4G with smartphones, with computers, with iPads that people have never had before. So rather than thinking I'm not sure if I can do this or if I'm technical, all that's irrelevant because in fact this is the first ever generation. If your kids do what you did, they'll actually end up broke. And that cannot be the way that we want the next generation to be so you must embrace this.

Paul O'Mahony:

James for example, made a million and a half pounds which is $2 million since November '18 following this process. This is a WhatsApp messages that he sent me as I was going on stage with Gary Vee and Russell Brand back last November just to get an update from him. And again, these are people who've been through the workshop, they've been through the three day and followed the system. And as I said the in person one we've no dates or obviously with the way things right now, and we have a massive backlog. However, we'll overcome that before we finish up the day.

Paul O'Mahony:

The first step is building your list, collecting people's information, give something away for free, very straightforward to do in exchange for your name and email address. We want to build our database, we make $1 per person per month, and we want to automate the process of selling the products, the top selling products that people want, whether they're yours or somebody else's, it doesn't matter. You can sell anything on Amazon, anything that's on eBay, any of the world's best training courses. Events like Tony Robbins where for example, the minimum price of a ticket might be $1200 and you get paid a three or $400 commission just for letting people know who follow him that Tony is coming to their town. You can create your own of course as well, you can publish your own books, you can launch yourself. And as I said earlier, you will save more by just changing the practices that I'm teaching you than you will ever invest in me in learning how to do this.

Paul O'Mahony:

And you can make . . . forget the savings. You can make some serious income from this. You make what's called high ticket sales, where you can make up to $4,000 from a single sale by promoting somebody like me where you literally click on a button, you enter your details, and we give you a link. That's the link when you promote and if anybody buys from that we pay you for anything that they buy.

Paul O'Mahony:

So when I wake up in the morning, let's take a look at how my day starts. I start looking at what sales came in. So each of these say £236.40 which is about I think 350 Canadian dollars, so I'm just going to say 300, 300, 300, 300, 300 300 300 300, Actually, I'm just going to say 3, 3, 3, 3, 3, 3, 3, 3, 3, 3,3, 3, 3, 3, 3, 3, 3, 3, 3, 3, 3, 3, 3, 3, 3, 3, 3. £116, £116, 300 Canadian, £116, $58 US, £116, and it keeps going. $58, £236, $997 997, 997, 997, three payments of 997. 997, 997, 997, 997, 997. You'll never get tired of saying 997, 997, 997, 997, 997, 997, 997, 997.

Paul O'Mahony:

How many of you think this might put a pep in your step in the morning, rather than meeting Starbucks or meeting coffee? Why? Because rather than looking what other people are doing on social media, rather than worrying about what other people think about you and what you should do. as Jack famously says, "What other people think of me is none of my business," and that could not be more prevalent in today's environment. Remember what the internet is, though? A systemized cash accumulation machine, and everybody should have one. Forget the naysayers. Never listen to people who give you free advice because it's worth every penny. Make sure who you're listening to has the type of income that you want to get to, not the type of income you want to move away from.

Paul O'Mahony:

This is a screenshot I took literally just before I came on here. Now, just to give you an idea. When everybody else is panicking about business going backwards, this is one of our click funnels accounts. One of six different click funnels accounts that we have. Where today so far $27,000 passively, yesterday, $26,000. So far in the last seven days, $60,000, the last four weeks $288,000. And our business from just this alone has gone up 50 . . . we've made 52% in a month of the entire year, because it's so easy for us to pivot, given what's going on in the current economy.

Paul O'Mahony:

So when everybody else is panicking, we're making what people would call lottery winning money in literally a single month. It'll be $300,000 by the end of Tuesday, by the end of the month. So it's your choice. You either decide to learn this and do this and get excited about it and make it happen. Or you think, "Interesting," and go back to life the way it was. For me, I can never . . . I said I'm so grateful every single day that I made that decision to not follow the crowd or follow the people. Because if you follow the people who have the results you don't want, you're still going to end up with the results that they have.

Or as John Assaraf says, if you continue to do what you always do, you're going to continue to get what you always got. And that's the crucial thing. We need support. We need to learn new things. It's not your fault, the results that you have today. That's how the system is set up. You can't learn how to get rich from broke teachers. And I can say that because my parents are teachers. You can't learn to run a business from lecturers who never had one. Today, you are earning whatever you're earning as a direct result of what you already know. What you learn after today will be the results that you get from what you start to do from today onwards.

Paul O'Mahony:

Today is a tipping point. Make sure you take that picture. If you decided already, that you're committed to move forward, the secret to success is this, do what the top sports people do. Do what the top business people do. They all pay for coaches all the time. Even Raymond is paying for me as a coach that will show you that you become very humble, the wiser you get you realize, the less you know, and you pay for coaches who pay for shortcuts.

Paul O'Mahony:

People that struggle with money use their time to buy money. People who have the money use their money to buy time. We need to switch the currency around, we need to pay for shortcuts. We need to be shown how climb on the shoulders of giants, see what they're doing, imitate it, copy, implement it. Success leaves clues, follow the system. It works every single time. All we're doing is giving people who are pre programmed to get rid of all their money, what they're looking for, what you get paid a commission every single time.

Paul O'Mahony:

This is how we and my team can help you. We do coaching and mentoring and we are going to run a virtual summit. We do not have a date announced because I know this question is going to get asked, the date has not been announced yet. But don't worry, even if you cannot make that date, we'll make sure we get you onto one or you can get a recording of it, whichever is your preference.

Paul O'Mahony:

You already took a picture of the three-day workshop. Which is now going to become virtual. So you can watch this from the convenience of your own home without flights, without travel, without hotels. And I'm also going to include my mindset mastery training to make sure that you can overcome the challenges that everybody is facing in the current environment so that you bounce out of this, that you see this at 2020 as the year when everything was reset, when it actually gave you a 2020 vision as to what it is that you want to achieve truly in life.

Paul O'Mahony:

I was walking down the street the other day and watching a dad with his kids, two kids, one on either side, and one child in front of him. And I actually had this thought where I said, "My God, so many people think that the dream is living at home and having more time with their children." And looking at their father, I realized this is actually his nightmare. He hadn't actually fully thought this through.

And a lot of people are questioning all of what they thought life's purpose was right now because we've been given this chance to take a pause to take a step back and see, am I going . . . there's only one thing worse than going in the wrong direction, and that's going in the wrong direction at speed. And so many people are doing that. We need to make sure that ladder is up against the right [boom 00:56:08]. As we just heard. So what I would suggest to you is get help.

Paul O'Mahony:

Luke, for example, here, he made $7,000. He said last week, "$8,000 for the first time next week. Who would have thought this was possible just a few months ago, I've already paid my parents back for the loan. They think I'm selling drugs. Lol." I had a call with him about five weeks ago, he made $2.3 million last year in 2019, starting from scratch following the process.

Paul O'Mahony:

Salman I told you, $210 in 11 minutes. But he's nowhere near Kiane who last October in the workshop made $13,000 in two days. This guy is 13 years of age. He is his child but kids can do it so you can do it too. Remember, this is why I'm so focused on helping kids and teens to do with because it's so simple.

Paul O'Mahony:

Forget outsourcing, start in sourcing. You've got people at home right now who don't even have homework to do, but they would love to get stuck into something like this. So they can start to build this business with you. The family that learn together, earn together. And I think you can massively improve everything you have from a financial perspective by deciding that you are ready.

Paul O'Mahony:

Actually, type into the chat right now, I'm ready. If you are ready take the next step, and start making dramatic changes. Take all of the knowledge that you're learning around mindset over these few days and investing and starting to apply it into something practical, where you can start making money or helping others and that's ultimately what this is about.

Paul O'Mahony:

And here is your invitation to come work with me. It starts on Monday at midday Eastern time. It's live, it's with me, if you can't make it, it will be recorded. There will be four more sessions then drip fed to you. That's a total value. These values are in US dollars. The investment that I will give you in a moment will be in Canadian dollars. So that's the total value of the five sessions of 997 dollars.

Paul O'Mahony:

Secondly, the virtual work shot that we talked about. Everything that you need to know, bringing you back together after you have received the training and already set up your business.

Paul O'Mahony:

Number three is the Opt-in page, we will create the technical side of things for you. If you're worried that you're not technical enough or that you think it might be challenging, no problem, we're going to hold your hand through the process, we even build the Opt-in page for you.

Paul O'Mahony:

Number four, we are going to give you an entire year's support of our help center, we have a 97% satisfaction rate in our help center. That's the thing I am most proud of in my business because we put so much time and effort into helping people our average clients 52 years of age, which will give you an idea of the level of support that we put into that.

Paul O'Mahony:

And then number five is all of the training that I'm going to give you. Everything from twitter, Facebook, how to rank your video on the first page of Google or YouTube, how to blog, how to build your list, how to find the perfect products to sell. How to outsource all of this to somebody else for $3 an hour. How to use LinkedIn, and lots more besides total value conservatively, there at $13,000. This is digital, you'll get lot of action . . . oh, sorry, login details to action it from Tuesday of next week after we have our call on Monday.

Paul O'Mahony:

Number six, I'm going to include the Facebook and Twitter ads training, which is online, as you saw for £2997, between a half thousand dollars that is going to be included. Also, you can immediately fast track yourself into maximizing your chance with cheaper ads that are out there right now to get amazing results.

Paul O'Mahony:

Number seven, if you've ever been interested in running webinars like what Raymond is doing, I've got a client who I showed what to do around webinars, he made $300,000 in 90 minutes, $500,000 in another hour and a half, $100,000 in 90 minutes. And he said, "Paul, I tell everybody about that advice you gave me and how I went from making one sale to 100k the next day. You changed my life man. Other than that business is great." That's $900,000 in six hours. The average family in the US spends $1300 a year on lottery tickets. Don't put anything around your finances down to hope or dreams anymore. The difference between a dream and a goal is a plan.

Paul O'Mahony:

Let's put a plan together let's make it happen. I have this training called Webinar Wizardry that I will include as a bonus for you that shows you step by step how to do this, whether you want to be the host, or whether you want somebody else to do this for you. And in the current environment that we're in, so many people could do with that skill set, have been shown how to take their business online and get in front of their own clients.

Paul O'Mahony:

And to make sure that you do this, I'm also going to include three one to one calls with me and my top coaches to show you how to make up to $4,000 per sale. Free personal calls, have your handheld through the entire process. That's a total value of 6K.

And I'm also going to help you out with your children or teenagers at home from next Tuesday. They get access to a half day online training, showing them how to become financially smart, how to start saving, how to grow up compound and how to start making a huge difference in their lives financially. Including the business plan for them that they can get started with straight away from Tuesday.

Paul O'Mahony:

So here's a list of everything you're getting the online virtual workshop, the live session on Monday, the Optin page done for you, access to the help center per year. Access to all of the training and the membership site. The webinar wizardry training which is worth more than your entire investment. Facebook and Twitter ads training. Three personal coaching calls with a lot more bonuses in there too. That's about $38,000.

Paul O'Mahony:

That ain't happening. But this was for sale when I launched it. It was 9,497 plus 127 per month. But I am going to do for you because I'm a really, really good friend of Raymond is we are going to go crazy. Not 20% off, not 40% not 60% off which will be 4k, you are going to get this for 1397 Canadian, which is the equivalent of around 997US. 1397 everything I talked about, it's aaron.com/social media. And I am going to do something crazy for those of you . . . as if that isn't crazy enough in the next five minutes here, if you go right now to aaron.com/socialmedia, I will personally do not just one but two one to one calls with you about your current business, your new business whatever it is. There's no expiry on this you can use them whenever you want aaron.com/socialmedia. This is just for the people to get in right away.

Paul O'Mahony:

I would personally work with you to fast track you. my daily rate is £10,000 or $12,000 per day. Two calls with me soon as you get your program implemented. And the second . . . sorry Raymond I'm just rushing on this. The other thing I'm going to do for you which is absolutely crazy. If you would like to bring a family member or a business partner with you, they get everything also two for one the entire program, two for one, no catches. They log in with your details and get access to absolutely everything that comes in the virtual summit. As Warren Buffett says investing in yourself is the most important investment you'll make in your life.

Paul O'Mahony:

If you cannot afford $1 19 per day to do this, you cannot afford not to do it. It's as simple as that. Two for one, two calls with me, if you're a business owner, of course, it's a write off against your company, and your money back guarantee. If you change your mind in the next week, for whatever reason, I will still give you the coaching calls, you will still get my blogging training. You still get on the three personal coaching calls, and you'll get your money back. That's even if you change your mind because I don't want you to buy this if you're not going to do it. I want to make it absolutely ridiculous, no brainer.

There's a list of everything that you have. I need to take a rest after this and just sit down, because I've never squeezed 100 minutes into 63 before. Thank you so much, Raymond for having me. It is as crazy as it sounds. Two one, two one if you get the entire thing for two people and everything that you can see there that barely fits into the slide. Go to aaron.com/socialmedia.

Raymond Aaron:

Well-

Paul O'Mahony:

Thank you so much, Raymond.

Raymond Aaron:

[inaudible 01:03:59].

Paul O'Mahony:

Thank you so much for the opportunity. I really, really appreciated. Wendy, Mike, everybody in your entire team, you were amazing. We appreciate it. If there's any questions for me, if there are time I'm happy to take.

Raymond Aaron:

There's no questions. We're over time. Paul, you were amazing. Thank you. Aaron.com/socialmedia and the people who get in the next few minutes, get those extra bonuses. This is the one I bought. This is the one I bought. I will be sitting beside you learning. Thank you, Paul. Thank you.

Paul O'Mahony:

Thank you, Raymond. Thank you, everybody. Take care. We'll see you on the program.

Conquer Social Media During Turbulent Times

Mari Smith

Raymond Aaron:

Never seen you so beautiful. Your smile is better than I've ever, ever seen. She is the Queen of Facebook. She knows how to monetize, that means how you can make money on Facebook. I don't want to give you a big introduction because we're a little late. Go.

Raymond Aaron:

Unmute yourself. Unmute yourself.

Mari Smith:

Thank you. Thank you. Thank you. Okay, excellent. And I'm sharing my screen. Can people see me as well on camera or are they only seeing my screen?

Raymond Aaron:

You and the screen. That's it.

Mari Smith:

Good. Good, good, good. Okay, I know there's a lag time in the group. Okay, cool. All right, friends, I got a few slides for you. Wonderful, wonderful, wonderful being here with you. I'm going to talk to you about social media best practices during turbulent times as we're calling them. It's a great awakening. That's what I think it is right now, great awakening.

Mari Smith:

Real quick because I always like to just pop a little slide in here in case you've never heard me before so you can get a sense of who you're listening to. They, the great they have called me the Queen of Facebook for about the last 13 years or so. I do work on and off with Facebook as a contractor. I inserted virtual there. I'm a globetrotting virtual keynote speaker. I'm a social media thought leader for over a decade. I do a lot of brand ambassador work. I care deeply with a passion about my peeps as I call them, my audience, my community. I'm Scandifornian. If you know, it's a wee accent there. I'm actually Canadian but Scottish. My parents are Scottish. I'm Scottish Canadian. Then I live in California since 1999.

So lovely to meet you. Wonderful being here. There's nothing I don't know about Facebook. I was just in a Facebook live on my page, and they made a major announcement yesterday, a lot of new things. So I'm going to cover a little bit of that.

Mari Smith:

So because ever since the pandemic, there's been a real oh my gosh, what do we do on social media. Is it okay to promote your business on Facebook and Instagram right now? Should you pull your ad campaigns? Should you completely change up your social media strategy? Well, let me answer those questions.

Mari Smith:

So guess what, the really good news for those of you who are savvy, if you were either advertising, you were before or you're thinking about it or you're brand new to advertising, there's never been a cheaper time to advertise because some major brand, a lot of businesses have pulled their ad campaigns. So that has made a big impact on the cost of ads. Ad costs are actually down by as much as 50%. Excuse me. So good news for us. Good news for us.

Mari Smith:

Now then the cool thing, friends, I'm actually going to be talking about there's two types of businesses that are needed more than ever right now, and this is my own philosophy, my own approach to this whole new world that we're in right now.

Mari Smith:

Number one, any product or service that enhances people's wellbeing on all levels, mental, physical, emotional, spiritual. If you are in that category, fabulous. People need to hear from you. It's fine to market and advertise, do organic and paid on social media.

And the second one, anything that enhances people's finances on all levels. If your product or service helps people save or make money or invest or cut costs or increase profitability or hire people that can help people grow their business, those are what I'm recommending. They are two main types of businesses that you really want to be doubling down on your marketing efforts right now.

Mari Smith:

So Facebook, Instagram, I predominantly focus on those two. I do quite a bit on Twitter as well. I don't do a lot on LinkedIn, keep meaning to, but LinkedIn's pretty awesome as well for all of your social media. And there's three key metrics. No matter what's in your watering can that you're looking to grow, three key metrics. This is across the board, no matter what times were in. You want to be measuring traffic to your website, offer, sales page, you name it, generating leads, and creating revenue. That is it. That is it.

Mari Smith:

So what happens is that people are often . . . They're like, "Oh my gosh . . ." Hang on, I didn't mean to stop sharing my screen. Let me go back to my screen. There we go. I thought it would go to my camera.

What often happens is that people get all caught up in what we call the vanity metrics. They're called vanity metrics or proxy metrics, and that is likes, comments, shares, reach, fans, you name it. All of that, even video views, those are important. They're a precursor to these three metrics, but they're not the be all, end all. You can't go to your CEO, your CFO and go, "Hey, we got 10 more likes today." They're going to be like, "Okay. Show me the money." But at the same time, there's a methodology, and I actually teach this full on method. I call it the Mari Method. I've been teaching it for many years, and I'm going to show you a little tip of it. And you can come into my different courses and programs. I'll show you where you can meet me in one of my most successful Facebook groups to get support and learn some of these teachings.

Mari Smith:

So the Mari Method is actually helps you to optimize both paid and organic predominantly using the power of video. So video is actually the most affordable and effective top of funnel content format on Facebook and really on Instagram as well. So that includes live, it includes recorded. Then what you do as you've done a live or you've uploaded a recorded video, and now you're going to go into ads manager and create what are called custom audiences based on people who have viewed your videos. And then you'll retarget them. The concept here is to lead people through a journey, lead them through a sequence, and you're not just trying to go, "Hey, buy my stuff, and click the button." And then people get frustrated and wonder why Facebook ads don't work. You've got to lead them through a sequence that gets them to know, like, and trust you.

Mari Smith:

And it does not always have to be you on camera. I'm totally fine being on camera, but a lot of people are not. And so there's great tools. The two that I use and recommend, one's called Wave.video, the other one's called InVideo.io, and you can create beautiful, professional videos in minutes using their royalty free stock content or your own. Upload from your camera roll, you name it. So really, really great tools.

Mari Smith:

Now why you want to focus on video is because Facebook is giving priority to video on both recorded and definitely on live. And many of you probably know that Mark Zuckerberg, CEO of Facebook, Founder, the mission of the whole company, which includes WhatsApp, Messenger, Instagram, Facebook and all the other things they do, Oculus and Portal and whatnot, to bring the world closer together. But look at this, friends, Facebook actually has a separate mission statement for video, and that is to, "Create shared experiences and a sense of belonging." What we're doing right here today with Raymond and all his friends and creating much more of a shared experience and that belonging through video. I know you're streaming on YouTube and into the Facebook group or using GoToWebinar. Live video is so powerful for creating that deeper connection with our audiences.

Mari Smith:

So right now as we're finding our way, all of us together, business owners and entrepreneurs or employees or if you're out of work right now, you're looking for opportunities. There's really, we're kind of in this . . . You've heard a lot of people say we're in the same boat, but it's like we're finding our way collectively. We're finding our way forward because there's only going forward. There's no going backward. Is that you've got to figure out what are my messaging.

Mari Smith:

If you're looking for work, you're looking for clients, you're growing your business, you're looking to get that traffic, leads, and sales, you want to embody these communication skills to help, to motivate your follower to take action. And that is direction-giving. Tell them what to do. Make it so clear, so clear, and ideally one call to action in your message, in your post or your email. One clear direction-giving action.

Mari Smith:

Meaning-making, this is a really important skill that helps people understand, and this is in terms of leadership in particular. What is the purpose of this? Why? What's in it for me? Why should I do that? What benefits are there?

Mari Smith:

And then the third one, which a lot of leaders are absolutely lacking, especially right now, is empathy. And that means that we can be in the shoes of our audience, of our customers, of our prospects. We can empathize with what they might be feeling right now. Now that is actually based on American professors Jacqueline and Milton Mayfield. It was just covered up there for just a second. And the book that they wrote on motivating language theory. Really powerful to know.

Mari Smith:

So if you can embody all three, not just one but all three in your leadership, in your communication skills, and your social media marketing messaging, it's going to make all the difference.

Mari Smith:

So this is what we want to be doing right now is building our community. So focus in on Facebook groups now more than ever, really important and with the video chat that Facebook just announced yesterday. Building community more than ever. Continuing with relevant offers, absolutely. Like I say, if your business falls into helping people's wellbeing and/ or helping them in anything to do with financial. Now if your business doesn't fall or the company you work for, whatever it might be, it doesn't fall into one of those two categories, that's fine. That's up to you to decide. But the point's here relevant. You seen the offer. You've probably been pitched like me with ads in the newsfeed that feels like people are tone deaf. They're oblivious or the flip of that, they're trying really hard to take advantage. They're actually trying to capitalize on this time right now, and you can feel the agenda of a leader. You want it to always be heart centered and focus on value, providing exceptional value no matter what. Those are really, really good best practices. Always relevant and always adding value.

Mari Smith:

Now then Zuckerberg has been saying for probably a couple years now that change is coming. Yeah, no kidding, Zuck, you knew. But what he's referring to in particular, see that padlock right there? This was Zuck on stage at the F8 Annual Developer Conference for Facebook just last year, April of 2019. Now he just streamed it live. He streamed his remarks live yesterday because obviously they're not getting together in person. But the big change he's referring to is the future is private. What on Earth did Zuck mean by that? He meant that they're doubling down on messaging, private messaging, private groups, stories, even though your stories on Instagram and Facebook people can see your stories publicly, but the conversations are private.

Mari Smith:

And so this was back in the day when we used to be able to gather. This is me speaking in front of about 800 people. One of the rooms at Social Media World. I got to keynote it last year in front of 5000 people, which is pretty awesome. So I love speaking. I love traveling. I love speaking. However, right now, what we're doing is this. I think this is Zoom. So we're getting together like this, and then, ta-da, yesterday, Zuckerberg just announced a Zoom competitor. They're called Messenger Rooms, and you can create a room for up to 50 people. And it's unlimited time. You can chat on video for as long as you want with up to 50 people. There's privacy in terms of being able to lock the room and only let specific people in.

Mari Smith:

I just did a live. You can go to my Facebook page at Mari Smith right over here, and you can find it right here. That one right there. Review of all the Facebook changes because there's a lot of them. They announced a lot of changes. Actually, I've got it pinned to the top right here. All the changes. The Zoom rooms. Excuse me, I said Zoom rooms. Whenever I say room, I think Zoom room. Messenger Rooms, Facebook live paid. They're doing paid Facebook live. Instagram lives are going to be saved to IGTV. Lots of great things. So hop over to my page after this and make sure you like and follow me and put it on see first. I'm definitely the place to get anything that's happening with Facebook, you'll find it on my page.

Mari Smith:

So these Messenger Rooms are going to be really powerful for us to connect certainly with our friends and family, but there could be some really cool uses in groups because you can do these rooms, these chat rooms, video chat rooms for up to 50 people in groups.

Mari Smith:

Now I think if I just have this right here . . . Yeah, I've got my screen shots are up right now. Yeah. So this is an example from Facebook where they're showing you this is not quite out yet. It's coming in the US next week and then all the other countries in the coming weeks. And they're showing here's a group of 21,000 members and showing how easy you can create a room. And then over here you can see there's multiple rooms. Wonderful ways to be able to connect with your audience in the rooms.

Mari Smith:

So my recommendations are absolutely combining the right message with that leadership, giving direction, helping people understand the meaning, and having empathy, making sure you're messaging is on point in both video and written. That you combine that with video. So you're doubling down on your Facebook groups. If you don't have a group right now, definitely start one. And for sure, friends, link your group to your page so that more people can find your group directly from your page. You can also interact in your group as your page. You just go to the groups tab on your Facebook page and you'll see up there there'll be a button that says link your group, and then you can join as your group and admin it. So that's a really good one. You can go live in your group. You can do all kinds of creative stuff. So many things you can do, and I'm happy to help you with that, anyone that needs support.

Mari Smith:

Talk to your audience more frequently. This is particularly right now in these turbulent times. Now you're probably like me, you've gotten tons and tons of emails form people you never knew you were on their list, and all of a sudden out of the blue they're messaging you in this crisis. But the point is right now more than ever, people need to hear from you with compassion, with empathy, with understanding. One of the posts I put out right away on March 12 was just, "How can I help you?" That was my subject line in the email. I got the highest open rate in a while. How can I help you? Just be of service.

Mari Smith:

I truly believe that right now is a great reckoning for businesses to stand out and people will long remember a year from now, two years, five years from now, they'll long remember the companies that had their back and that were helpful and that were kind and were considerate and gave them tremendous benefits, payment plans and pick your price and differed payments, whatever it might be, and just really have their backs. So I think that it's really important to talk to your audience.

Mari Smith:

Broadcast with Facebook and Instagram live more often. I saw a stat go by the other day that Instagram live has increased by 70%. 70%, big growth in live. So it's good timing that Facebook just mentioned all of these updates. Facebook live with Raymond . . . It's so funny. Raymond, I saw you doing your . . . You did a short Facebook live yesterday on your profile, and you obviously brought up the button to say go live with. My guess is it's still a bit buggy. But you can do the live with, Facebook live with is coming back, and I know it's a very popular feature.

Mari Smith:

Now then, as I just mentioned, I go live regularly. Love to go live on my page. I have a whole strategy on how to increase views and how to . . . See, this one's got 96,000 views. That one has a budget behind it. Working with one of my ambassador partners, and really, really powerful new way, relatively new, it's been out for years. But Facebook is determined to become the next generation digital streaming television. So if you're not doing video, you're absolutely going to be left behind. You got to do video. It does not have to be all live. I recommend live if you can. Live gets six times the engagement than regular video. If you don't like being on camera, you can do recorded videos, I mentioned earlier, with Wave or InVideo.

Mari Smith:

Whoopsies.

Somebody unmute themselves. Thanks.

Mari Smith:

And then watch parties. So those are really powerful. You probably seen that option where it's got the little popcorn icon, and you're like, "What the heck is that," or maybe you've participated in one or you've always wondered what it was or maybe you tried hosting it. But watch parties are like having movie night. You can actually pick any public video, including your own. You do it in a group page profile, and you can create a playlist. And you host a video or a series of videos, playlist of videos for your audience. And as it says here, people are 800 times more likely to comment on videos in a watch party than just watching it solo. So you just put a little title on it and add your videos. Really powerful tool.

Mari Smith:

All right. So about to finish up here. Martha Beck, one of my favorite . . . She's a life coach and leader. She's had a column in the Oprah Magazine for 20 years, and what she says is, "The world truly needs emotionally intelligent leaders more than anything right now." That goes back to those three leadership skills that was mentioning. More important than ever to be able to give clear direction to explain the meaning of things, of why something's important, why people should learn from you, and why you're asking them to do something, why you're asking them to sign up. And then having that empathy. Empathy goes hand-in-hand with what Martha's saying here, emotionally intelligent. Guess what, Martha actually said this 10 years ago at the California Women's Conference in 2010. Wow.

Mari Smith:

Now speaking of Martha, I want to show you her ad on Facebook because it jumped off the screen to me. I thought it was so well done. I study ads. I help people to run their own ads. My clients can often get incredible, much, much lower cost per lead. We just helped someone lower their cost per lead from $60 per lead down to $10 per lead for a really, really high end, exclusive audience. So with Martha, she's not a client. I'm just using her example. I saw this ad where it said, "Thriving in Turbulent Times." I love the white water rafter guy here, and what caught my eye, friends, is holy moly, an ad with 1100 shares. And I loved how she started out with, "Dear friends," like she's writing a letter. This is a moment we'll remember for the rest of our lives. I showed you the full ad because people often ask me is long copy okay in an ad. It's fine. Absolutely. The answer to that is absolutely.

Mari Smith:

That took you to simple landing page where you signed up. You registered for her 74-minute free video. She didn't do all that nonsense of . . . I shouldn't say nonsense because I know it works for some marketers. But it wasn't like pick your time and you have to wait and then you forget and then you don't watch the video. But she just gave you it right away. It wasn't like one of those pick your time webinars. She wasn't trying to be a live webinar. But it's an hour and 15, and it was so good. It was incredible value. I took notes. I rewound it. And she gave you the transcript and the audio download. What was so good, and she made an offer, sure. She's getting people to sign up for her program, which I think was like $300 or something. I think the door's closed now. But it was so good. It was really on point, and you probably seen a number of people doing offers that are really on point.

So my invitation to you, you want to learn more from me and get support, find out about my courses and my trainings, how you can join my mastermind and whatnot, is come on over to my Social Scoop Facebook group. I mentioned that earlier. It's one of the easiest ways. You can see it's linked to my page here, and definitely like and follow my page. It's the one with the blue check. Facebook.com/MariSmith. And then with my Social Scoop Group, you'll see it's really, really . . . I think we have 9600 members, and it's one of the best ways to get incredible support, peer support, and also access to me and my team. You can also get it at the socialscoop.com.

Mari Smith:

And when you come over there, I do have a gift for you if you choose to, if you want to. It's optional. But if you let me know your email, I will send you . . . In the group, you'll go to join the group, and I will send you my free gift. It's my Top Five Facebook (and Instagram) Marketing Challenges with Solutions. So that is my gift to you when you come on over and join my group.

Mari Smith:

So with that, my friends, I believe that I have managed to catch you up on time, and we've got a couple spare minutes. So I can either do some questions or you've got other folks coming on.

Raymond Aaron:

No, you're still on for three more minutes. You did catch me up. I'm really, really grateful. My takeaway was heart, that they want empathy, they want answers, they want reality; they don't want salesmanship.

Mari Smith:

Yes.

Raymond Aaron:

That's what people generally want even though high pressure salesmanship still works unfortunately. But in this time, in times when people are frightened, it's even more important to be heart-centered, and you totally are. I love that we're in Transformational Leadership Council together, and I love that we get to see each other in normal times on vacation twice a year. And I love how wise you are on Facebook, on social media, and how gentle you are. Very sweet and unusual combination.

Mari Smith:

Oh, Raymond, that's so kind of you. Can I just say one quick thing?

Raymond Aaron:

Sure.

Mari Smith:

I have to tell everybody here that my claim to fame is I taught Raymond how to tweet. That was like 2009 or something. 2008 even.

Raymond Aaron:

Yeah, we all have to learn sometime.

Mari Smith:

Way back in the day.

Raymond Aaron:

I got to learn from the Queen.

Mari Smith:

So long ago.

Raymond Aaron:

We have time for one question. Francis, can you pull out one wonderful question?

Mari Smith:

That'd be awesome. I love questions.

Raymond Aaron:

[inaudible 00:22:39] is better than ever today.

Francis:

Yes. There we go. [crosstalk 00:22:44]. What's the best Messenger marketing tactics?

Mari Smith:

Oh, Messenger marketing. Francis, that's a great question. So people might want to check out ManyChat. ManyChat or Mobile Monkey. There's a couple of different great platforms out there. They're third party. You do have to pay for them. They've got free. Go ahead and take it for free, test drive. But with Messenger, because as I mentioned, Zuckerberg said the future's private and they're doubling down on private messaging. Then the idea here is that when someone goes to communicate with you on your page, you can even put a little widget on your website. And then you send automated answers back, and you also have permission to broadcast to them. So

ManyChat, M-A-N-Ychat.com, and then my friend Larry Kim, he has one called Mobile Monkey. You can take them both for a test drive.

Mari Smith:

And then, yeah, there's a lot of different experts out there that really specialize in that as a niche, and you can just test it. Doesn't really quite work like email marketing. It isn't about blasting. It's more about conversations and helping people find answers. And then directing them to where you want them to go.

Raymond Aaron:

Very sweet. Very, very sweet. No wonder you're world known.

Mari Smith:

Thank you.

Raymond Aaron:

You are. Okay. Thank you, Mari. I'm honored that you're on our show.

Mari Smith:

My pleasure. Thanks for having me.

How Coaching Helps During Turbulent Times

ORBIT Members –
Glenn Edwards, Lisa Stringfellow,
Miha Bavec, Gregor Hočevar,
Ruth Verbree, and Manny Bains

Raymond Aaron:

I have an inner circle of coaching clients. I'm just going to introduce why it is called Orbit. Orbit is a level that the electron lives around . . . please mute yourself guys. Mute yourself please. When an electron whirling around the hard center of an atom, it gets excited. That means when energy is added to it, it jumps, it jumps to a higher orbit but it doesn't jump slowly. It doesn't jump gradually, it jumps instantaneously. So Isaac Newton was wrong and Albert Einstein was right when he came up with the idea quantum physics. Quantum means a particle. So if you get insufficient energy, the electron does not jump. If you get 99% of the energy, the electron does not jump. When you get a hundred percent of the energy required, it instantly jumps, not slowly. Physicists can see the electron at the lower orbit. They can see it when it is at the higher orbit, but it's never in between.

Raymond Aaron:

It's a gigantic instantaneous jump. So I've named my inner circle, my most powerful coaching program, the Orbit, and I'm very restrictive. I allow very few people in and I work with them as often as they wish. It's a six-month program and it's really powerful and I've invited some of my Orbit members and I've given them this instruction before, but I wanted to say it again, do not sell the program. This is not a sell thing. I just want you to tell your own experience what your problems were before, what happened to you, what's your biggest highs were, the biggest takeaways. I'm going to get rid of my video because there's six that I've invited and after I invited six Orbit members, I found out that only six spaces going to be on the screen. So I'm taking mine off and please just share the screen. Just go for it. Whoever wants to talk first, go for it.

Glenn Edwards:

I'll go first. My name is Glenn. I'm an award-winning author, a motivational speaker and personal coach. I met Raymond, January 15th of this year to speaker's course he put on and I joined Orbit that weekend. It's been transformational, changed my life incredibly. I've written a book already, I coauthor with Raymond, Les Brown and Dr. John Gray. Raymond and I are actually co-writing right now with another book. So that's just incredible to be able to doing that fast with Raymond. The older group, you guys are incredible. Raymond you're incredible, amazing coach, just phenomenal keynote speech I've got already. Just changed my whole format of where I'm going with my life.

Glenn Edwards:

I've got two construction companies and just to alter my life that fast and go off in this direction, it's the second biggest passion I've ever had and I can't think Raymond enough, can't thank the Orbit team, the Raymond Aaron Group, everybody has been phenomenal. The support is amazing. Raymond I can get a hold of you anytime I want. You even got back to me during this weekend you put on. So incredible. I won't take up much more time, but thank you to everybody and to you Raymond.

Raymond Aaron:

Glen, can you hear me?

Glenn Edwards:

I can.

Raymond Aaron:

Yeah. Good. So one of my rules for Orbit members is, never add time. One of my coach, Dr. Nido Qubein, who's the president of High Point University taught me speed of implementation and Dr. Joe Vitale, who was on earlier today has written a book called "Money Loves speed." Money Loves Speed. So what is this whole thing about speed? Why have I been so caught up in it? Why have you progressed so fast? What is it about speed?

Glenn Edwards:

Like you say, don't add time. Do it now. Whether it be the phone call, the book, the speech, advertising yourself, promoting yourself, or reaching back for help from you. Why delay it? Why put it off, do it now, act now, follow your passion and go after it.

Raymond Aaron:

Yes, and Glenn did text me while I was hosting this World Prosper Summit, and I was able to look down, see it, come up with an answer and text him back within a minute while I was hosting this show. I do anything for my Orbit members. Can you believe how much you've changed? Like give us an example of how much you've changed.

Glenn Edwards:

Oh, it's incredible. The day we decided to do this and go to Orbit and join you, it was an emotional day. You remember that I literally broke down in tears because it was the second biggest passion I had in life. Obviously, hockey was the first. Between you and the staff and everybody there just incredibly transformational. It just brought up that passion. It's just, it pours out of you. You can't help it and I can't wait to see where this goes. I can't wait for the next sport to come out. I can't wait for this COVID thing to end. Actually, I'm being an infection control expert I'm part of this now. So even this I'm putting myself out there. I did something today and put it out, promoting myself and trying to help people really.

Raymond Aaron:

Brilliant. Thank you, Glenn. Thanks for-

Glenn Edwards:

Thank you. Thank you so much.

Raymond Aaron:

Lisa, we had the most recent coaching call I did was with you?

Lisa Stringfellow:

Yeah.

Raymond Aaron:

You also got a bonus that my amazing wife was also [inaudible 00:05:41] coaching you.

Lisa Stringfellow:

She was. She's amazing.

Raymond Aaron:

So Lisa was an employee for a fabulous job earning a good income and suddenly she gets an idea from me about what to do based on the lockdown. Do you want to tell us the story?

Lisa Stringfellow:

Oh, we were on a coaching call, I decided I wanted to use the time we have now in the lockdown to improve my life even more than I already have done. You and your wife, actually, both of you had the idea for a new business. I've started writing a book on the subject. I put together some proposals and hopefully we'll be rolling it out next week to some of my local businesses. Sorry guys I don't really want to tell you what it is yet till I've rolled it out, but I'm really excited. I think it's really really going to work. But within a half hour coaching call, we had a business plan, a proposal, the name of it, what to call my employees, everything done right then on the call.

Raymond Aaron:

Deliciously branded, like a really clever name for her [inaudible 00:06:59], a wildly clever name for the company. It's a perfect business. It's an elegant business and she's already got a major government office wanting to be her clients. They called her, this is amazing. She will likely replace her entire income, her salary income from this one job and it's a permanent income. Oh, I'm so proud of you Lisa. You also-

Lisa Stringfellow:

You know . . .

Raymond Aaron:

. . . You also understand speed of implementation.

Lisa Stringfellow:

Yes.

Raymond Aaron:

I don't [inaudible 00:07:36] work any delays [crosstalk 00:07:37]. Go ahead.

Lisa Stringfellow:

Without your help though, I wouldn't know about speed of implementation and I'd still be thinking about it and thinking about what I could do rather than having it all done in that half hour coaching call.

Raymond Aaron:

I know, I know. So-

Lisa Stringfellow:

I know.

Raymond Aaron:

. . . So I tell all my clients, "Don't you dare start a business unless you're branded." Because if you're not branded, you're just drowning in the sea of sameness like everybody else and you'll have competitors. But when you're branded, you'll have no competitors because you stand out. So I told her, it's going to take you a week to get everything ready and get your logo and all that in the meantime, write a book and finish it in a week. "Yes sir." So she's writing a book in a week. It'll be amazing, it'll brand her and she's in a whole new life. A whole new world. We don't know where this change will [inaudible 00:08:28].

Lisa Stringfellow:

No, and while Glen is hoping that the lockdown will be over soon. I'm like, "Yeah, it's been so good for me." So, I don't want it to end.

Raymond Aaron:

Okay, let me pick on Miha. Miha, you can't see him. You can see how tall he is because he's sitting down. [crosstalk 00:08:52] It gets hard at anybody in the world and he lives in one of the tiniest countries in the world, Slovenia and he is a master he's revered in Slovenia as a business coach, a business leader. When we started working together, life started changing for him. I remember scaring the daylights out of you. Now he speaks with a bit of an accent, a little hesitant and he said, "Raymond, I want to be a professional speaker." I said, "Good. I have a speaking gig for you in front of 300 people, 10 days from now." "What!" He went crazy, but he did it and he was the star of the show. He was so humble and so humorous. People were in endeared by his gentle accent. It was, anyways you tell your story Miha.

Miha Bavec:

Oh, thank you Raymond. First, I'm really happy to be here to be part of this event today. So it's wonderful to know and of course you remind me of this story. It was really tough thing for me, but this was the first time I met with your idea of don't add time. I never learn before English in my life, I only learn German all the time. When you give me only 10 days to be there in Toronto, in front of 300 people, it was a really hard time for me. So I'm really thankful for this because I stretched myself so much. It's hard to explain, but it's true really and I know that you helped me to create a lot of stretching in one year.

Raymond Aaron:

Also I invited you into the home of some of my most famous brands. Want to say a bit about that?

Miha Bavec:

Yeah. There are so many great experiences here in Orbit Group, but being able to be [inaudible 00:10:58] those special peoples. This is really amazing. I couldn't imagine other options to be there, to meet these people. So it was really, really great to meet Jack Canfield in person. You'll see him, today I believe and he's really great person. But if you can meet with him in his living room in California, oh, this is amazing really. The second experience was when we visit Dr Nido Qubein. It's a great, great, great guy in North Carolina. It was so powerful to be there really. I will remember this days for all my life. This year, you arrange a meeting with Bob Proctor and I can remember this dude. He's a person, such a great person. Such a great energy. I was there [few hours 00:11:56]. He surprised us and he'd spend time with us, I sit one meter from him in the front [inaudible 00:12:02]. I really enjoyed this one life experience really.

Raymond Aaron:

Thank you Miha. Some of the benefits of the Orbit coaching program is the coaching itself, the wisdom that you get from me, the insights, the degree to which I speed your life up, but the other meeting and being in the home of some of my world famous friends, when you're in the home of somebody world famous, you get caught up in the energy, get caught up in the feeling, in the charisma and the aura and you're never the same again.

Miha Bavec:

This is a special level of experience. You can read the books of those people or observe them on the stages or online events, but it's quite stomping different when you meet with humans in their home because you really speak with the person, they spend the time with you and you can feel the space and his energy and it's really beautiful.

Raymond Aaron:

Thank you. I keep the number of Orbit members small to about six because I give them so much. They can contact me anytime for a five minute coaching. They can text me any time for an immediate text reply and if they wish a full half hour coaching session, they go through my assistant to book it. But they get as many coaching sessions as they wish for the entire time. Of the six people who are in it now, two are from Slovenia. How is that possible? The tiny little country and it's so beautiful.

Raymond Aaron:

When I got off the airplane and I was taking the ride to the hotel, I was dazzled by how clean it was, how pretty it was and how relatively crime-free it was. I asked Miha, how comes it's crime-free since everybody knows everybody. You can dare do anything on [inaudible 00:14:07] because everybody knows. So the other Orbit member from Slovenia is Gregor and Gregor is a master at athletics and he has written a masterful book on how to treat your clients like royalty and let's find out from Gregor. Say hello and tell us what you learnt. Tell us your big highlights.

Gregor Hočevar:

Oh, hi to everybody. I'm honored to be on this summit, along these big names and that's thanks to you Raymond because one thing when I joined Orbit is also that I can attend all of your workshops, seminars and so on for free. So it's included in, and also got to meet Bob Proctor, Jack Canfield like Miha did and all the other people. That's one of the things why I joined. The other was also writing a book, which branded me and since then everything went the other way. So I was out of the sea of sameness and everyone knows now who I am and what I'm about. So that's thanks to you. Also I have nonstop, like I can reach you whenever I want. I can call you, I can text you. One time it was late, here it was 11.30 my time, and I needed you instantly and you just answered me, "Okay, call me right now." We discussed about one thing and you solve my problem, which is amazing and that's why I joined. So to have constant access to you and to other stuff that you offer.

Raymond Aaron:

Thank you. Yes. Not only are you access to me at all times and as you said, and I forgot to mention, you get any event that I hold at VIP. It's, yes I just love doing that. For Gregor, he had a legal problem with his neighbor, which we solved. I gave him the negotiation tactic which he used, and he runs a family business which we helped improve and he wanted to get into a brand new business of being a speaker. We worked on that, whatever he wants, I've guided him and it's going and he's happy. You're a good guy, Gregor.

Gregor Hočevar:

Yeah. Maybe just to say this, it's not only about business stuff. You can talk with Raymond on the personal level or sports level. It doesn't matter. He can uplift you if you're in a bad mood or anything else. So it's not only the business wise or the product he offers. So he's really there for you or me. So I got a lot of it.

Raymond Aaron:

Thank you, Gregory. That's very sweet. Ruth, Ruth, our motorcycling mama.

Ruth Verbree:

I want to take-

Raymond Aaron:

I don't think she'd ever given a speech before. I don't think she'd written a book before. Now she's been on several stages, she's written a book, she's positive, she's developed new products, she's selling her products, this is a whole giant new life for you. Tell us.

Ruth Verbree:

Thank you so much, Raymond. I want to thank you for this opportunity to share the stage with these wonderful renounced speakers on a virtual summit. Thank you for doing this. I am so excited to let you know that Raymond's always got back. Raymond is a friend, a mentor, he's my coach and he has helped me in so many areas of my life. He has helped me become an international speaker and not only that, an award-winning author. I met Raymond five years ago now and I first signed up for his 10-10-10 Program to write a book. As soon as he started talking about writing a book, my husband looked at me and said, "This is for you," and I ran to the back. I was so excited and I didn't add time. I didn't and in four months I had my book.

Ruth Verbree:

I started rebranding myself and then what I did is, I just loved Raymond's teaching so much that I kept going for more. I wanted more, I was learning and growing and I just had to jump into the Orbit program because Raymond just has a world of information. He is such a wise man and he has helped me in my personal relationships. He's helped me in my business. He's helped me in my spiritual life. He has helped me in every aspect of life and here's the biggest thing he's helped me with, he has helped me learn how to take my greatest barriers and turn them into my greatest successes. I will be forever grateful for that, Raymond and it's true you can reach him anytime you want. You just text him and he's there. If you phone, he'll answer, he just treats us like royalty, like Gregor's book.

Ruth Verbree:

But he is such a wonderful teacher, a guider and because he's taught me so much, I now have two online programs and I'm helping hundreds of people through my programs, helping women learn to love their bodies, helping people learn to develop their mind, body and soul, just because of my greatest barriers. I've turned them around into successes. One of the greatest barriers for me was that I had a poor body image and many women can relate to that. But Raymond has taught me to turn that around and now I have an online program. So Raymond, I am forever grateful. If people want to check out my program, they can. They can go to my Facebook page, it's

Ruth Verbree. But Raymond, you are a star. You are a star of my life and I just can't thank you enough. The Orbit program has meant everything to me. Thank you, Raymond.

Raymond Aaron:

Okay. You pitched something, but it wasn't clear Ruth for . . .

Ruth Verbree:

It's Ruth, just they can check me out on Facebook, Ruth Verbree.

Raymond Aaron:

Oh, spell it. They don't know how to spell it.

Ruth Verbree:

It's V as in Victor, E-R as in Robert, B as in Bob, R as in Robert, E-E. V-E-R-B-R-E-E. Thank you Raymond.

Raymond Aaron:

Yeah. Good. If you're going to promote yourself, you better do a good job.

Ruth Verbree:

That's right.

Raymond Aaron:

Listen. I'm coaching them even here and now I don't want to say finally, I just want to say the next is a really special character because it is the only father-son, Orbit coaching client I have. I'm just going to talk about his dad for a second, because I love his dad so much. In one of my classes, and they can attend any of my classes at no charge, his father [Rob Banes 00:21:23] got so turned on that he stood up and he just blurted out, "I am reactivating my PhD program.

I'm going to finally become a PhD." He started his PhD and stopped like 95% done with 5% to go. He stopped because he didn't have a compelling enough topic that he truly loved to finish his PhD on. He didn't know what to do his dissertation on, and he didn't just want to get a PhD for nothing. He wanted to make a difference and, in my program, he found his love.

Raymond Aaron:

He went back to the university, they approved him restarting, they approved his topic and he's going for his PhD. I'll tell you, Orbit members from around the world are going to be getting together and dancing at his PhD graduation party because we have each other's back. We love each other so much at every event, all the Orbit members just glam together and take pictures of each other. Manny, Manny on our last coaching call, he said, "Raymond brand me. Brand me." Branding takes months. You don't just brand somebody. I said, "Well, what's your special? What is good about you? What stands out? What do people say about you?" He said, "Well, people like to be around me. They like to be in my group." I said, "So they're in your group and you're the head of the group. So what do they call someone who's head of a group?"

Raymond Aaron:

I said, "Mayor Manny," and it stuck. He is mayor Manny and he loves it and I love it. I like calling him mayor Manny and he loves speed of implementation. He quotes the term speed of implementation more than any other Orbit member. So mayor Manny, tell us whatever you wish to say about the impact of the Orbit program on you. Unmute yourself. Unmute yourself.

Mayor Manny:

. . . Thank you, Raymond, and thank you for that amazing introduction and thank you for making history and getting me to share the stage with all of my fellow Orbit members. That's great. I'll never forget the day me and my dad enrolled in Orbit. It was last summer and we're actually seeing Raymond in Los Angeles and my father was actually receiving an award for his book that he coauthored with Jack Canfield and a few other people, but he was getting an award and we go there and we're like, "Okay, we're just going to come here, get your book and go. We're not going to sign up for anything." Next thing you know, we're in Orbit and we're like, "Okay." We don't even know next thing we're in Orbit and it has been a crazy, amazing ride, ups and downs and it's been crazy.

Mayor Manny:

I've written two books since then and Raymond has actually helped me brand myself. I actually had this idea why I wanted to brand entrepreneurs through film, but I didn't really have a direction for it. It was just in the idea stage and Raymond helped me actually develop the marketing for it and I actually have my own program, the rising star movie experience, where I'm branding entrepreneurial through film and actually creating documentary films. Just signed an agreement where I'll be going to India to film. So when this is over, I'll be going to India and filming my first international project. I'm coaching people all over the world and did a workshop last weekend and I had people from three different countries. If you were to ask me a year ago, would this ever happen, I would have told you it's crazy. I think that the thing with a coach is that it just cuts the learning curve.

Mayor Manny:

Raymond has done years of wisdom. He's downloaded all of this information and he's just so open to give it to me so I can get to where I want to go faster. That's the whole point of a coach is to help you get you to where you want to go faster. So my dad has had breakthroughs, my dad was drinking for, he wasn't an alcoholic, over 50 years. One coaching session with Raymond, I'll never forget in Cancun and it was done. He hasn't even touched a drop since. Me and dad had become closer than ever. We were already close, but we're so much closer now, our bond is stronger than ever, and we're just learning off each other and I'm just so grateful for Raymond. Just really transforming my life night and day and teaching powerful business and marketing principles and on branding. It's just truly amazing. I'm just so grateful for you, Raymond. Thank you so much. It's been amazing.

Raymond Aaron:

So I feel it. I really feel it from you. So can you imagine, here he is in the short time he's been in the Orbit program, he's suddenly become a professional speaker, he suddenly become a seminar leader with people from three countries in the world coming to his events. From his heart, he's always wanted to make movies and he didn't know how to monetize it. He didn't know what to do. He had the technical ability, but not the marketing ability, not the entrepreneurial wisdom and now he's got a brilliant name, rising star, the name of the movies that he makes for you. It's about you. It's autobiographical about you and it promotes you.

Raymond Aaron:

He's got a new business, deeper relationship with his dad, cheering his dad on to get his PhD. His dad used to have a glass of wine over dinner for 50 years. I looked at him and he said, "Raymond done, it's over." Last time I spoke to him, he said, "It's not that I'm trying to quit." He said, "It's done. It's just done." Talk about speed of implementation. So these are six of my Orbit members. The lifetime total is only about 11 or 12 because I keep the active members to about six. So, I love you, I'll never forget you. You uplift my life. You're some of my dearest, dearest friends. [inaudible 00:27:16] Oh-

Mayor Manny:

ORBIT, there's a family within this too. I didn't just adopt Raymond, but I'm with this, my ORBIT family and whenever I have a problem, I can lean on my ORBIT family and that's just another tremendous bonus of this.

Ruth Verbree:

We do love you [inaudible 00:27:34].

Gregor Hočevar:

It's funny that I have to travel 5,000 miles to meet my friend from Slovenia, which is 220 kilometers away from me. So it's amazing [crosstalk 00:27:46]. It's amazing what we have to do to meet someone who is actually on our backyard.

Raymond Aaron:

This is a completely unexpected benefit. The Orbit members love each other so deeply. They are willing to help each other so intensely at any time. I didn't expect it. We have a WhatsApp Orbit only chat group with maybe 12 people on it. It is still heavily [inaudible 00:28:15]. People share anything they wish and everyone else congratulates them. It's so beautiful. It has uplifted me maybe more than it has changed those special to me. I'm going to tell you the tuition and this is not a big sell because I only love very small number of people in it, and if it's more than you can afford, then it's not for you and there's no discounts. For half a year, it's US $50,000. For half a year it's US $50,000. For one and a half years it's $75,000. So for a half year, it's $50,000 for one and a half years, it's $75,000.

Raymond Aaron:

Very few people get accepted, way more apply than I accept even if they have the money, I don't accept them because I want people who are really serious. People who are going to go for it. People who are coachable, I need you to be coachable. So if you're interested, the place you go is just aaron.com/coaching session, aaron.com/coaching session. Choose your time slot and me and one of my staff will be in touch with you. Aaron. com/coaching session. Just spell Aaron correctly, because if you get that wrong, that's the IQ test. You can't get here. A-A-R-O-N.com/coaching session. So we're exactly on time. Wow. You are wonderful Orbit members. Everyone says goodbye. Goodbye. I love you.

Everyone:

Goodbye.

www.ingramcontent.com/pod-product-compliance
Lightning Source LLC
Chambersburg PA
CBHW060048100426
42742CB00014B/2739